CALVIN: A GUIDE FOR THE PERPLEXED

CALVIN: A GUIDE
FOR THE PERPLEXED

PAUL HELM

t &t clark

Published by T&T Clark

The Tower Building
11 York Road
London SE1 7NX

80 Maiden Lane
Suite 704, New York
NY 10038

www.continuumbooks.com

British Library Cataloguing-in-Publication Data
A catalogue record for this book is available from the British Library.

ISBN-10: HB: 0-567-03201-9
       PB: 0-567-03202-7
ISBN-13: HB: 978-0-567-03201-0
       PB: 978-0-567-03202-7

Typeset by Newgen Imaging Systems Pvt Ltd, Chennai, India
Printed on acid-free paper in Great Britain by MPG Books Ltd,
Bodmin, Cornwall

To

David and Maria Avren

and

Alan and Carolyn Winter

I have a natural love of brevity

Inst. III. 6. 1

How very minute a portion of divine wisdom is given
to us in the present life

Inst. III.2.20

CONTENTS

PREFACE

My main aim is to let Calvin speak for himself. I concentrate on the 1559 edition of *Institutes*, which Calvin justifiably regarded as his theological masterpiece, carefully revising it through a number of editions. He thought that it provided the theological key to his voluminous *Commentaries* and other writings, and so it does.

Apart from providing a brief biographical setting to the point where Calvin arrived in Geneva, and a few remarks about the circumstances of his death, the only other references to Calvin's life are incidental. In this way the reader is invited to concentrate on John Calvin's ideas, chiefly theological but sometimes philosophical ideas. Where there is a philosophical aspect or implication to the theology, I have tried to discuss this in terms of its historical setting. Readers who wish to pursue the philosophical connections further are invited to look at the author's *John Calvin's Ideas* (Oxford University Press, 2004) as well as *Calvin at the Centre* (Oxford University Press, forthcoming).

I have not attempted to say something about everything, but I have concentrated on those issues that are central to and characteristic of Calvin's thought. The approach to these issues is intended to be constructively critical, with attention being paid to the meaning and coherence of the ideas, and to areas of internal tension. I've tried to write clearly and to avoid anachronism and over-reliance on the benefit of hindsight.

Among the sources of perplexity with Calvin, at least in the popular mind, are his attachment to the idea of predestination and his connection with the execution of Servetus. I have said something about each of these, but there is much more to Calvin than these, for he is one of the great theologians of the Christian Church. I hope this short book will help its readers to appreciate why this is.

In studying Calvin I have come to be in debt to many people but chiefly, in the present work, to Oliver Crisp who kindly read the book in manuscript and has been a great help in many ways. It was he who reminded me that the book is intended to be a guide for the perplexed and not a perplexing guide, and I have tried to remember this. Thanks also to Angela and Alice who have become used to having John Calvin as a permanent house guest.

CHAPTER 1

ORIENTATION

CALVIN THE MAN

John Calvin is generally acknowledged to be one of the great doctors of the Christian Church and a 'world figure'. This book aims to consider the intellectual side to his life, to see how his ideas moulded his theology and spirituality, and how they also contributed to the formation of what came to be known as 'Calvinism', an outlook that has deeply affected and influenced what we refer to as the modern world. This chapter provides an introduction to that task, an 'orientation'.

John Calvin was born in July 1509 in Noyon, France, the second son of Gérard Cauvin (as the family was called in those days) a church official. The family lived in the shadow of the Cathedral. Initially his father destined him for the priesthood, and he was trained (in Paris) first in Latin grammar and then in philosophy. In 1525 or thereabouts, his father changed his mind and arranged for John to be trained as a lawyer. He made this change because the law paid better than did theology as, of course, it still does. So at around seventeen Calvin moved to Orleans to study civil law, in effect a branch of church law, the civil law of a Christian state. He never studied theology, though he may have been required to gain some theological knowledge as a part of his education in the law. His father died in 1531. Moving with some student friends to Bourges to be taught by the Renaissance scholar Andreas Alciati, Calvin himself began the life of a scholar, learning Greek and rhetoric and coming increasingly under Renaissance influences.

Sometime around 1529–30, in circumstances that are not at all clear, Calvin also came under the added influence of the nascent

Reformation movement in France and was converted. Throughout his life Calvin wrote little about himself. Unlike his mentor Augustine he wrote no *Confessions*. But what we do know about him is significant. In his Preface to his *Commentary* on the Psalms, comparing himself to the Psalmist David he wrote,

> But as he was taken from the sheepfold, and elevated to the rank of supreme authority; so God having taken me from my originally obscure and humble condition, has reckoned me worthy of being invested with the honourable office of a preacher and minister of the gospel. When I was as yet a very little boy, my father had destined me for the study of theology. But afterwards, when he considered that the legal profession commonly raised those who followed it to wealth, this prospect induced him suddenly to change his purpose. Thus it came to pass, that I was withdrawn from the study of philosophy, and was put to the study of law. To this pursuit I endeavoured faithfully to apply myself, in obedience to the will of my father; but God, by the secret guidance of his providence, at length gave a different direction to my course. And first, since I was too obstinately devoted to the superstitions of Popery to be easily extricated from so profound an abyss of mire, God by a sudden conversion subdued and brought my mind to a teachable frame, which was more hardened in such matters than might have been expected from one at my early period of life. Having thus received some taste and knowledge of true godliness, I was immediately inflamed with so intense a desire to make progress therein, that although I did not altogether leave off other studies, I yet pursued them with less ardour.[1]

As these words suggest, Calvin was a timid and retiring person but also excitable and, later on, bad tempered, which was something he deplored in himself.

This is part of the only autobiographical account of any length that we have from Calvin. Two or three things are worth noting. First, he saw himself to have been exalted (in retrospect of course, for he had no such ambition) to the position of 'a preacher and minister of the gospel', not as a professional theologian. In fact, he came to despise the term 'theology', equating it with unprofitable speculation. It is 'true religion' not 'theology' that he came to see himself as promoting. He was not an 'intellectual', interested in ideas for their own sake, though he had a formidable intellect; he was rather a Christian person who devoted his talents to the service of the church of God. Second, he believed himself to be in the hands of God, directed (as he believed all of us are) by God's 'secret providence', secret in the sense that the outcome of God's direction is presently unknown. For though he, Calvin, intended one thing, unknown to him God intended another. Finally, he tells us that he was 'converted' from the excesses of the Catholic church of his day and received instead a 'taste and knowledge of true godliness'. What Calvin means by this, I believe, is not simply that his allegiance changed from the Catholicism of his birth to the Reforming movement, a change made (say) for political or tactical reasons, but because he saw Protestantism as the nurse and guardian of 'true godliness'. Some have believed that these autobiographical remarks were deliberately contrived. But there seems to be no good reason to prevent us from taking them at face value, as Calvin's accurate recollection of a pivotal event in his own life.

Since this present study of Calvin is not chiefly biographical, the other phases of his career leading to his arrival in Geneva can be briefly noted.[2] Identifying himself with the Reforming, evangelical wing in France he moved back from Orleans to Paris in 1531 and published his *Commentary* on Seneca's *De Clementia* at his own expense in 1532.[3] No doubt through it the young Calvin sought to gain the academic recognition that he had craved. It is essentially a Renaissance, humanist production, though on a theme of concern to evangelical Christians who were anxious to be recognised as the legitimate Christian church in France, and so sought the 'clemency' of the King. Calvin touched on the theme of clemency in his Preface to the *Institutes*, in 1536, addressed to King Francis I of France. Whatever his ambitions may be been in writing the *Commentary*, it had a cool reception.

Around this time Calvin was implicated in the so-called Cop affair. Calvin's friend Nicholas Cop delivered a rectoral address in the University of Paris, possibly written by Calvin, which was regarded by those who heard it as heretical. Calvin was implicated, his rooms were searched and he and Cop fled Paris. Soon after he became involved in what is usually called the *placards* incident, in which posters condemning the Mass were prominently displayed in many French cities, and arrests and executions followed. As a result of these upheavals Calvin moved to Basel, a centre of the Reformation, where he began writing the book which was to be the first edition of

3

the *Institutes*, a modestly sized *apologia* for the evangelical faith that was structured on Luther's *Catechism*. After a year he went to Italy, to the ducal court at Ferrara where, it has been suggested, he became a secretary to the duchess, Princess Renée of France. By now he was a clearly identifiable member of an evangelical and Reforming group and once again had to move on. He went back to Basel and then to France. The Edict of Lyon of May 1536 granted 6 months grace to heretics before they were required to be reconciled to Rome. Calvin seems to have taken advantage of this, and after winding up his family affairs with his brothers Antoine and Charles he left France again, this time for Strasbourg. The party had to divert through Geneva because of troop movements. While there, he was immediately searched out by Guillaume Farel, who was leading the Reformation in the city.

> Wherever else I have gone, I have taken care to conceal that I was the author of that performance [the *Institutes*]; and I had resolved to continue in the same privacy and obscurity, until at length William Farel detained me at Geneva, not so much by counsel and exhortation, as by a dreadful imprecation, which I felt to be as if God had from heaven laid his mighty hand upon me to arrest me.[4]

So it was somewhat against his will that he became a teacher in the church. His influence on Geneva rapidly grew, even though he was exiled for a time due to disagreements over the speed of reform in the city. After his return, Calvin's Geneva quickly became a beacon for Protestant dissidents and refugees (especially from France), and through his ministry, correspondence and above all his writings he became the most influential of the second generation of the magisterial (as distinct from the radical) Reformers.

It is his concern to fulfil the office of a minister of the gospel that led to his own immense literary output. The centrepiece of that work is undoubtedly his *Institutes of the Christian Religion,* which went through numerous editions, reaching its definitive shape in 1559. As we have noted, it began as a modest work of catechesis but became more elaborate as Calvin's own thought matured and his desire for 'order' in Reformed theology increased, even though he continued to refer to it as a 'compendium of doctrine'.[5] On top of this, he incorporated material from the various controversies that he became engaged in during his Genevan years. These debates, often bitter and intense, were chiefly with more radical thinkers (e.g. over the Trinity, the person of Christ and predestination), with Roman Catholics and with his fellow Reformers (e.g. over the work of Christ and the Supper). Calvin came to regard the *Institutes* as a kind of theological key for Christian ministers, allowing him in his *Commentaries* to do without elaborate theological excursuses (which were a notable and wearying feature of contemporary commentaries). This enabled him to keep his comments on the biblical text brief and terse. 'I love brevity', he once remarked. This arrangement is in rather sharp contrast to his practice in the elaborate Seneca *Commentary*.

> For, if I mistake not, I have given a summary of religion in all its parts, and digested it in an order which will make it easy for any one, who rightly comprehends it, to ascertain both what he ought chiefly to look for in Scripture, and also to what head he ought to refer whatever is contained in it. Having thus, as it were, paved the way, as it will be unnecessary, in any *Commentaries* on Scripture which I may afterwards publish, to enter into long discussion of doctrinal points, and enlarge on commonplaces, I will compress them into narrow compass. In this way much trouble and fatigue will be spared to the pious reader, provided he comes prepared with a knowledge of the present work as an indispensable prerequisite.[6]

It is their brevity, combined with Calvin's genius as an expositor, his sensitivity to the text and his good judgment, that account for the *Commentaries'* abiding value. Alongside them were published several notable series of sermons, taken down in shorthand by the remarkable Denis Raguenier, and, of course, numerous controversial writings on grace, free will, providence, the person of Christ, the Trinity and the like. So Calvin had a number of different audiences. We shall refer to the whole range of his output, including his letters, in the chapters that follow.

Scholars have debated the extent to which Calvin was a Renaissance man. He was undoubtedly greatly influenced by that movement, having the ambition, before his conversion, of living out the secluded life of a Renaissance scholar. As we have seen, such a career wasn't to be. Yet the effect of the Renaissance did not leave him. It is to be seen in his *ad fontes* approach to Scripture, in his direct, personal style, his rhetorical cleverness and in his dialectical stance. While he could argue the point as well as anyone (as can be seen in his various polemical writings and the corresponding sections in the *Institutes*), he saw as his primary audience not only the citizens of Geneva but also the rising generation of Christian ministers, particularly those French, English, Scottish and Italian ministers and students who took refuge in Geneva. His approach was warm, typically using the first person plural, and his rhetoric aimed at *persuasio* rather than *demonstratio*.

Although, as we shall see, he was far from dismissive of the work of the mediaeval scholastics, his style was, in general, somewhat removed from that of the mediaeval *disputatio*. In the *Institutes* and the *Commentaries*, Calvin took it for granted that the author and his intended audience were on the same side. His aim was to imbue his sympathetic readers more deeply with the principles of Reform by informing and ordering their grasp of biblical religion and thereby firing them up. By contrast, in his polemical writings he could be fierce, dismissive, sarcastic, rude, relentless.

It is partly because of Calvin's personal style and pastoral motivation that the *Institutes*, though a great work of systematic theology, cannot be regarded as a textbook in theology. Another reason for this is that the *Institutes* was planned (and continually retuned and re-focussed in its various editions) as an instrument of the Reform. It is therefore an 'occasional' work, attending to those matters that in the author's judgement were then imperilling the Christian faith. Its treatment of topics is for that reason rather uneven. So the sole authority of Scripture is there, and justification by faith 'alone' (Calvin insisted on that word) is also there, together with a dismissal of an *ex opero operato* view of the sacraments. The centrality of Christ as the sole, sufficient redeemer, our Prophet, Priest and King; the bondage of the will to sin, and especially Calvin's strong sense of the unmerited grace of God, ring out throughout the work. As a consequence, he provides a withering polemic against the very idea of human merit and the supposed power of free will. Book IV sets out at considerable length an ecclesiology very different from that of the Roman Church.

But Calvin is a conservative by temperament, a 'catholic', and so matters not controverted at the Reformation are left pretty much alone. So (for example) divine simplicity, creation, the metaphysics of the Trinity and of the person of Christ are largely left undisturbed. They are agreed items, theological commonplaces. Calvin has an intense desire not to be sidetracked, to keep his eye on the main point.

When doctrines such as the Trinity and the Person of Christ are discussed and elaborated, this is often because Calvin reluctantly sees the need to rebut the claims of the radical and rationalistic wing of the Reformation. And where a central doctrine of the faith is endorsed, as is the case with the Trinity, what is distinctive about his treatment is not doctrinal innovation or fine-tuning but his view on what the distinctive Christian approach to understanding and utilising that particular doctrine ought to be. So if some theological dogma is not treated at length in the *Institutes* it would be unwise to conclude that Calvin does not endorse it or value it deeply.

These remarks may apply, I believe, to the much-discussed question of Calvin's attitude to natural theology. Did Calvin think it necessary to prove that God existed? If so, what proofs did he favour? The ontological argument of Anselm? The cosmological arguments of Aquinas's Five Ways? Why does he not discuss these issues in the *Institutes*? The matter has been a source of great controversy among Calvin scholars. Some, such as T. H. L. Parker, have thought of Calvin as a fideist in the Barthian manner.[7] Others, such as B. B. Warfield, see a few remarks on natural theology in Book I of the *Institutes* as indicating approval of natural theology.[8] Perhaps the answer is that there is little or no discussion, because Calvin broadly endorsed one then-current attitude to the proofs, that it was possible to prove God's existence but not necessary to do so in order for belief in God to be justified. Was this the point of his reference in the *Institutes* to what he calls the 'common proofs' of God's existence and his mild approval of them?[9] Natural theology was not the main issue of the Reformation, so he was cautious, though not sceptical, in his attitude to it.

Calvin's conservatism is also seen in his frequent appeal to the authority of Augustine, acknowledged on all sides to be *the* Father of the Church, or at least the Western Church, and to a lesser extent to Bernard of Clairvaux. The last thing that Calvin wanted was to be thought of as an innovator. But his use of the Fathers was not a front, and to Augustine and Bernard he was doubly indebted. He leaned on them time and again in their expositions of grace and will, and (in the case of Augustine) for much else, and he was glad to have their authority to endorse views which he believed were biblical but which the Christian Church in his own day had largely spurned and supplanted. So Calvin was far from being a pure Biblicist: he had due regard for the conciliar and patristic tradition of the church, though as subordinate authorities, subject to the supreme authority of Scripture.

Calvin's general stance is to see Christian doctrine as essential for the promotion of true *sapientia*, wisdom, rather than as providing *scientia*, theoretical knowledge. The *Institutes* begins with the words, 'Our wisdom, in so far as it ought to be deemed true and solid wisdom, consists almost entirely of two parts: the knowledge of God and of ourselves'.[10] Wisdom, the fear of God, the orientation of the self to God, is the chief thing. Therefore sound doctrine matters, but it is not an end in itself. It is more important than that. It provides the sinews of true religion. Hence Calvin's abhorrence of speculation – not because it is not possible to speculate about religious and theological matters, but because to do so is to be distracted from the main plot. Only rarely is Calvin dragged into matching a speculation he objects to with one of his own.

CALVIN AND CALVINISM

The study of Calvin must not be mistaken for a study of Calvinism. In the final chapter we shall briefly consider the wider impact and legacy of Calvin and the development of Calvinism, but until then it is important that the two are kept separate. There are a number of reasons for this, some obvious enough. John Calvin is an individual, one human being developing in a particular context. Calvinism is a movement, one that became a worldwide influence which, once the Reformed faith was almost completely snuffed out in France, was carried forward chiefly through the medium of the English language and to a lesser extent, of Dutch. Calvin died in 1564, but 'Calvinism', the 'Reformed Faith', lives on, changing and developing as a theological and cultural strand of the modern world. The relationship between Calvin and Calvinism continues to be modified as 'Calvinism' and the Reformed Faith change. To confuse Calvin with Calvinism and to suppose that when one is considering Calvin one is also considering Calvinism constitutes a kind of category mistake, like confusing Plato with Platonism, or Aquinas with Thomism, or J. S. Mill with utilitarianism. In this book, we are principally considering the thought of Calvin the man and not Calvinism the movement.

A second reason is that the relationships between Calvin and Calvinism are rather complex. Even beginning to consider these raises a number of questions each of which would require separate treatment, but which are often confused or conflated together. Restricting our attention to the ideas of Calvin, to his theology, here are four such questions. No doubt there are more. First, and most obvious, was Calvin a Calvinist? That is, was his theology as his followers developed it simply and solely the theology of Calvin? This is a question more about Calvinism than about Calvin. Was Calvinism so faithful to Calvin that it did not deviate from his theological position by a scintilla, or hardly at all, or not in any substantial sense? Is the history of Calvinistic theology the mere repetition of Calvin's own theology? A 'Calvinist' of a later era, Jonathan Edwards, offers one answer to the question:

> I should not take it at all amiss, to be called a Calvinist, for distinction's sake: though I utterly disclaim a dependence on Calvin, or believing the doctrines which I hold, because he believed and taught them; and cannot justly be charged with believing in every thing just as he taught.[11]

Here's another issue. The term 'Calvinism' draws attention to one individual. But the wider and continuing Reformed movement, the Reformed faith, as it came to be known, or Christianity in its Reformed expression, was in its earliest form the child not only of John Calvin but of an entire team of Reformed thinkers and activists. For example, Heinrich Bullinger (1504–75), the author of the *Decades*, who was especially influential in England; Martin Bucer (1491–1551), to whom Calvin himself was greatly indebted during his years at Strasbourg; the Italians Jerome Zanchius (1516–90) and Peter Martyr Vermigli (1500–62), trained in scholastic philosophy and theology to an extent that Calvin was not, were both friends and correspondents of Calvin. And others include, though now largely forgotten, Calvin's colleague Guillaume Farel (1489–1565), his friend Pierre Viret (1511–71) and Theodore Beza (1519–1605), who became his immediate successor in Geneva. All these thinkers and preachers, and many more, contributed to the Reformed faith as it rapidly developed in the middle years of the sixteenth century. What of John Knox (1514–72) or of Zachary Ursinus (1534–1583), the author of the influential Heidelberg Catechism? Were they all 'Calvinists' as Calvin himself was?

Suppose we keep our eyes on the central theological teachings of Calvin, and leave aside much that was, to begin with, a part of Calvinism, its ecclesiology for example, or its views of the relation between church and state, or its social thought or its attitude to culture. A further question here is, is the theology of Calvin (in this narrower sense, a sense perhaps coextensive with the topics treated in the first three Books of the *Institutes*) *consistent with* that of the 'Calvinism' in a similar narrower sense? Did the later theology, for example, deny or repudiate or ignore important elements of Calvin's theology? Suppose that we could satisfy ourselves that, as far as these things can be judged, Calvin's theology is *consistent* with that of later Calvinism, using (perhaps) as a standard of such consistency the appropriate parts of later confessional pronouncements of the Reformed faith such as the Canons of the Synod of Dordt or the Westminster Confession of Faith. Then a further question is, was the later theology (as measured by these parts of these confessional documents) *entailed by* the theology of Calvin? Did Calvin's thought contain within it elements which the later Calvinism deduced and elaborated more fully in a way that Calvin himself did not, perhaps because he did not have the time or the energy or the insight to do so?

All these are legitimate questions, each of them the subject (as it happens) of intense scholarly debate in the last generation or so. For what it is worth, my own view is that the later, confessional Calvinism was broadly speaking consistent with the theology of Calvin (but also with that of many other early Reformed theologians), certainly to an extent that is often denied, but that it is going too far to claim that Calvin's theology entailed these developments and certainly much too far to suppose that Calvin himself *intended* them! The point of drawing attention to such questions here is to show that they involve complex issues which take us far beyond the subject of this study, which is John Calvin's own theological ideas.

One besetting danger is anachronism, the attempt to answer questions of a later time as if Calvin could have foreseen them. Calvin lived into his mid-fifties, spending most of his adult life in Geneva, in the middle of the sixteenth century. He was phenomenally busy with one thing, the furthering of the Reformation. Just as it is unhelpful to our understanding of Calvin's theology to offer a translation of it into modern categories, to correlate it with modern issues, so it is equally misguided to try to get Calvin himself to address questions that cropped up long after his death and that he did not have an inkling of. Would Calvin have been in favour of the modern environmental movement? What about abortion on demand? What side would Calvin have taken on the later Amyraldian controversy? Did he believe in definite atonement? The covenant of works?

The value of controversy, whether conducted by present day academics or in the life-or-death way at the time of the Reformation, is that it demands of those who engage in it that they think not only about what their own view of some matter implies but also about what it does *not* imply. Controversialists necessarily have to think both sides of the question at issue, to say what they believe and also what they do not believe, or why they view some issue with indifference. Calvinist theology has enjoyed its share of such controversies: the extent of the atonement, the nature of the divine decrees and their relationship to each other, the character of divine foreknowledge, whether human ability (or inability) limits human obligation and the relation of nature to grace, for example. Although we may form a view on what the Reformed faith (as it is expressed in the last edition of the *Institutes*, for example) implies on the matters just mentioned, it is quite another thing to try to imagine what Calvin himself did think, or might have thought, on controversial issues which erupted long after he was laid to rest.

However, we must be careful not to take this circumspect attitude to excess. We are not to think that because Calvin lived 500 years ago the lapse of time has hermetically sealed off his thought, that we now cannot understand it as it was and reach a reasonable degree of objectivity about it. To take up such an attitude would be to adopt modern forms of academic scepticism and relativism. We must not so stress the importance of taking a person's ideas in their context that 'context' becomes a kind of cocoon that we cannot ever hope to break into with understanding. Calvin's thought is not written in a bygone code that we cannot crack. We are not engaged in an effort to 'read' a set of texts the original meaning of which is ever lost to us. We must, of course, be open to the possibility of legitimate differences in interpretation, that Calvin's words may bear various meanings. But this is not the same as saying that we are free to give to the material whatever meaning we choose because the meaning that it had for Calvin and his original circle is inaccessible or that now it is only of antiquarian interest.

As we have noted, Calvin is one of the great doctors of the church and one of the fountainheads of the Reformed faith. To some he is a hero, a father figure, someone that they want, or need, on their side. Others demonise Calvin, painting his thought in lurid colours and perpetuating myths. We need to be aware of these tendencies so as to avoid them ourselves. It does not detract from Calvin's greatness to do so.

Here are some instances of appropriation or rather, as I believe, of misappropriation. In the 1930s, in the context of the rise of the Nazi Party in Germany and its creation of 'German Christianity', a sort of religion of the German nation, the theologians Karl Barth and Emil Brunner engaged in a furious exchange over the legitimacy of natural theology. The idea was, presumably, that 'German Christianity' was being presented by the Nazis as a form of natural theology or natural religion and the question became: is any form of natural theology legitimate? Can German Christianity be dismissed root and branch?[12]

The details of this, or its ongoing theological significance in contemporary theology, do not concern us. What is interesting about this fracas, however, is that both Barth and Brunner, two outstanding twentieth century Reformed theologians, sought to gain John Calvin as an ally. So Barth trenchantly held the view that Calvin repudiated natural theology and therefore would have repudiated German Christianity. Brunner took the rather more nuanced position that Calvin endorsed forms of natural theology but nevertheless would have repudiated that form of it that was expressed in German Christianity. A natural reaction to all this is, What does it matter what Calvin thought? More fundamentally, how could we possibly know what Calvin, dead these four centuries, would have thought? Why did Calvin's views matter? They mattered because he was, in the eyes of Barth and Brunner, the fountainhead of the Reformed tradition and therefore someone worth having on one's side.[13]

Here is another example. There has been a strong tendency among some interpreters of Calvin, arising from the work of the Dutch theologians Abraham Kuyper (1837–1920), and Herman Bavinck (1854–1921), to emphasise Calvin's view of 'common grace'. That is, as they understood it, the view that the viability of human cultural activity is solely the result of God's general goodness and not of innate and autonomous human capacities. Such interpreters have often made a principled opposition between natural law, which they believed that Calvin eschewed, and common grace, which they believe that he embraced. 'Nature' thus understood is regarded by the Calvinistic proponents of common grace as an area of human life that is (it is alleged) autonomous, self-propelled and where God and his grace are not needed. Rejecting this picture of the relation between nature and grace (which is thought of as mediaeval), Kuyper and Bavinck argue that the whole of life is so infected and skewed by sin that the restraining and gifting of God to human society and culture are not to be explained in terms of the workings of nature, but they are the result of God's 'common' or general grace.

But Calvin shows no sign of making such a sharp antithesis between 'nature' and 'common grace'. Natural law and the sense of equity on which it is based – important themes in Calvin's ethics and his understanding of human culture – are the gifts of God. They are not untouched by the Fall, nevertheless their continued efficacy is the result of God's goodness in preserving human life and its powers. It is untrue to say that for Calvin the divine image in man was blotted out.[14] It was spoiled, and its integrity was lost. But it does not follow that everything about it was lost as well. When God engraved the moral law on the minds of men, this was a gift to them, an act of undeserved favour, of grace. Insofar as this continues, though affected by sin, the gracious gift remains. We shall discuss these matters further in Chapter 6.

Some scholars have wished to distance themselves from Calvin by attributing to him extreme views that he did not in fact hold. Thus Alasdair Macintyre has claimed that

> Calvin too presents a God of whose goodness *we* cannot judge and whose commandments we cannot interpret as designed to bring us to the *telos* to which our own desires point; as with Luther, so with Calvin, we have to hope for grace that we may be justified and forgiven for our inability to obey the arbitrary fiats of a cosmic despot.[15]

And Keith Ward perpetuates this myth when he asserts that 'One cannot satisfactorily ground the finite universe in a God whose values are wholly contingent, like Calvin's God, who could choose anything at all as a value, at the fiat of his arbitrary will'.[16] Note the phrases, 'the arbitrary fiats of a cosmic despot', 'the fiat of his arbitrary will'. But Calvin is at pains repeatedly to stress that in his view the will of God cannot be separated from his justice, and that what he commands is not arbitrary or whimsical, but rooted in his goodness. 'We, however, give no countenance to the fiction of absolute power, which, as it is heathenish, so it ought justly to be held in detestation by us. We do not imagine God to be lawless'.[17]

CALVIN, THEOLOGY AND PHILOSOPHY

During controversies over the Trinity and justification by faith in Calvin's day, there were some who said that the disputants should only use the very words of Scripture. Although, as we shall see in Chapter 2, Calvin had a strong view of the sole authority of Scripture in matters to do with the faith, he does not agree with such biblicism.

> If they call it a *foreign* term, because it cannot be pointed out in Scripture in so many syllables, they certainly impose an unjust law – a law which would condemn every interpretation of Scripture that is not composed of other words of Scripture . . . But in regard to those parts of Scripture which, to our capacities, are dark and intricate, what forbids us to explain them in clearer terms – terms however, kept in reverent and faithful subordination to Scripture truth, used sparingly and modestly, and not without occasion. Of this we are not without many examples.[18]

Calvin proceeds to defend the principle that our thoughts ought to be scriptural, but that, especially in controversial contexts, they may be expressed in words that are not to be found in Scripture. In a similar way he defends the addition of the word 'alone' in 'justification by faith alone', because, although not to be found in Scripture, it faithfully captures the meaning of Paul.[19] On the other hand, he strongly objected to the introduction of the word 'merit'.[20] More often than not such introduced terms are philosophical or logical, or ones used by philosophers, such as 'substance', 'nature' and so on. Calvin inherited this way of thinking from the tradition and did not demur. They take him into the realm of philosophy.

This world of philosophy was not entirely foreign to him. We have already seen that Calvin had training in philosophy and law but not in theology. Some have supposed that he was taught by the Scotist (and Scottish) philosopher John Mair, or John Major (c.1467–1550), but there is no hard evidence for this. What is clear is that Calvin was far from the purely 'biblical' theologian that he is sometimes represented as being. It is true that he repeatedly and scornfully dismisses the 'speculations' of the philosophers, but it would be a mistake to think that this amounts to a blanket condemnation of philosophy. The 'speculators' in question were not ancient philosophers, nor even scholastics, but principally the *sorbonnistes* of his own day, bent as they were on obstructing the work of Reform in France.

Calvin's own attitude to philosophy, and to the relationship between theology and philosophy, is more mixed. On the one hand, he praises the acuteness of some philosophical distinctions. In his treatment of the soul, for example, he says this: 'I admit, indeed, that what they ingeniously teach on the subject is true, and not only pleasant, but also useful to be known; nor do I forbid any who are inclined to prosecute the study'.[21] Although not in favour of philosophical speculation himself, he does not forbid it for those who have the time and talent. He utilises evidence from Cicero for a universal *sensus divinitatis*, taking the Roman philosopher to be providing empirical support for the Apostle Paul's claims in Romans 1.[22] Calvin thinks that the ability to reason is among the gifts of God's common grace. He follows Augustine very closely, and so adopts many of his philosophical positions, though occasionally he distances himself from the more Neo-platonic concepts and ideas that Augustine employed. Despite condemning 'Stoic fatalism', he nevertheless uses Stoic elements in his exposition of predestination. As we have already noted, he adopts the traditional understanding of God as simple and timelessly eternal. Calvin himself is a pronounced mind–body dualist and uses the language of Plato to characterise the soul's present relationship to the body, several times calling it a 'prison-house', though he also finds biblical precedent for such language in II Peter 1.13–14, and Job 4.19, and II Corinthians 5.2.[23] He adopts several philosophical distinctions current in mediaeval philosophy, for example, between the necessity of the consequence and the necessity of the consequent in his treatment of providence, between essence and accident in his account of the effect of the Fall on human nature, the use of the Aristotelian fourfold view of causation to illuminate the atonement, the *totus-totum* distinction in discussing the unity of Christ's person and so on.

In general, Calvin has a higher regard for the value of philosophical discussion in metaphysical questions than over moral issues. He thinks that when ancient philosophers discuss moral questions, the moral incapacity of human nature, for example, the 'greatest geniuses are blinder than moles'.[24] In their estimate of the powers of human nature we see 'the great darkness of philosophers who have looked for a complete building in a ruin, and fit arrangement in disorder'.[25] The philosophers had no conception of the Fall and its moral consequences and so mistook the abnormal for the normal.

So we may say that Calvin has a rather eclectic attitude to philosophy, using the concepts, argument and attitudes of philosophers of various schools – Platonic and Stoic in particular – where he believed that they were profitable in elucidating the faith and preserving it against misunderstanding, but turning his back on them when their work was 'unprofitable' or where it endangered some biblical teaching. But there is one area in which Calvin was firm and positive. Whatever his general caution, he could not countenance the presence of self-contradiction, of logical incoherence, in Christian theology. As insistent as he was on divine sovereignty, his view never approaches that of Descartes that even the necessary truths were subject to the power and will of Almighty God.[26]

From the time of the Apologists, and more especially from Augustine onwards, Christian thinkers have used philosophy to 'understand' their faith. They thought that the Apostle Paul provides precedent in his reasonings with the philosophers of Athens (Acts 17) as well as in his controversial debates in his letters. In some cases such 'understanding' has meant the offering of rational support for the faith, proving the existence of God, for example, or the necessity of the atonement. But more generally it has meant using the tools of philosophy to elucidate the biblical testimony, to draw out its implications, to preserve it against distortion and caricature, and to harmonise one part of Scripture with the others. Augustine's struggle to understand God's relation to time, and the consequences of this for a view of creation, in Book XI of the *Confessions* and elsewhere, is a prime example. In Anselm's case 'understanding' is taken further. It implies a proof of some central Christian claim without relying at all upon the authority of Scripture: in the *Proslogion* he argues that God *must* exist, in the *Cur Deus Homo* that there *must* be an atonement, and this atonement *must* involve the Incarnation of the Word. Aquinas' great *Summae* as well as many of his other writings, heavily reliant on the newly translated Aristotle, must be understood as notable achievements in this 'Faith Seeking Understanding' tradition.[27]

Where does Calvin stand? Part of the difficulty of answering that question is that while he repeatedly defers to Augustine, he hardly ever even mentions Anselm or Aquinas, or others in that tradition, by name. This silence is puzzling. In the case of Anselm, it is fair to say that Calvin would regard his reliance upon unaided reason as excessive, because it has the effect (even if not the intention) of taking us away from the authority of the text of Scripture and of adopting a kind of a priori attitude to the dogmas of the faith. Calvin would demur in general from this stance, even though his view of the atonement has strong Anselmian themes, and though he offers some of Anselmian reasons for holding it, as we shall see. Calvin's relation to Aquinas is more intriguing, for if we use several of Thomas's views as a kind of template, then many of Calvin's own positions can be seen to have a Thomistic pattern, even though with significant differences. This is another bit of evidence that Calvin automatically accepted many of the thought-forms of the late-mediaeval world.

There are several reasons why Calvin was not to be a mainline exponent of the 'Faith Seeking Understanding' tradition, however. They have to do with his personal situation and his growing sense of what he was called by God to do. He came to see himself as one who was called by God to seek the renewal of the church by revisiting the scriptural foundations of the faith and reforming the current abuses of Christian faith and life by them. He was tirelessly busy with all that the project of the Reformation involved. As a result, Geneva became one of the great hubs of Reform. It is not too much to say that he was consumed by these issues, and so had no time for that quiet scholarly reflection that, at one stage in his life, he so much craved.

Another reason has to do with his strongly held belief that human capacities were weakened by the Fall. This made him cagey of trusting unaided reason. Finally, he has a deep sense (deeper, perhaps, even than Augustine) of the hiddenness of God's purposes, his 'secrets' and of the incomprehensibility of his dealings with the human race. God has chosen to reveal his saving purposes in Christ and has for this purpose 'accommodated' himself to us. But – by implication – there was much about himself that God had not revealed and perhaps even things that he could not reveal. The idea of providing an understanding of all such matters by demonstrating their consistency, or at least by demonstrating that they were not inconsistent, with what he has revealed is beyond our meagre capacities. It is not worth attempting.

So Calvin is very much in the 'Faith Seeking Understanding' tradition and drew upon it for his own theological formulations. Yet he himself, because of his personal situation, his strong sense of the noetic effects of sin upon human reason, and his distrust of speculation, was committed to the work of theology proper. So we may say that although Calvin was not a philosopher, and did not have a philosopher's temperament, yet in his work he was receptive to philosophical ideas and arguments, using them where he could, in a rather eclectic way.

However, in recent years the theological and philosophical position of Calvin has been appealed to by 'Reformed' epistemologists such as Alvin Plantinga and Nicholas Wolterstorff. They see him as having philosophical insight, as giving precedent to what (because of him) is currently referred to as 'Reformed' epistemology. As they have developed this epistemology, they have made a strong appeal to what Calvin has to say about the *sensus divinitatis* as a kind of precedent for their own views.[28]

But now we are beginning to get into Calvin's epistemology, the topic of Chapter 2.

CHAPTER 2

THE KNOWLEDGE OF GOD AND OF OURSELVES

ACCOMMODATION

John Calvin does not have a theory of religious language, such as a doctrine of analogy, or an emotive theory. He is not very interested in how our language about God works, even though he is a master of style himself. The language that he is chiefly interested in is not our language about God, but God's language for us, God's language in Scripture. For although he is fully appreciative of the humanness of the Bible, (though, of course, living in a 'pre-critical' era), he thinks that these human documents are, by divine inspiration, divine documents too.

Similarly, he is not much interested in God as he is in himself, but as he is towards us, not in the immanent Trinity so much as in the economic Trinity, not in the metaphysics of the person of Christ so much as in the fact that as God-man he is our divine Mediator. In a similar way, he is not interested in a 'theory of God' or a 'philosophy of God' but how God is to us.

God communicates to us chiefly in the language of Holy Scripture. That language is all right as it is. We, though fallen, are created in the image of God, and so we possess innate receptors for that language even though these are skewed and perverted by sin and so need the instilling and illuminating of the Holy Spirit. Nevertheless, though our thinking is affected by sin, we remain fitted to receive God's word in a way in which cattle and chimpanzees (say) are not, and God's word is suited to us. His accommodation to us has its climax in the Incarnation of the Son.

So Calvin's key idea about language, the language of divine revelation with which he is principally concerned, an idea which I think he gets from Chrysostom,[1] is that in using human language God *accommodates* himself to us. He comes down to our level by disclosing himself to us in language that is suited to our condition, to our straitened circumstances as time-bound and space-bound creatures. For Calvin 'accommodation' is usually a term of grace, the sovereign grace of the gospel as it is made known in the word of Scripture and the Incarnate Word. Sometimes he uses 'accommodation' for God's grace in a less central sense, as when God deals with men and women as he finds them. If his people under the Old Testament are barbaric, then God suits his word, particularly the ethical standards which he announces that he requires of them, in a way that is tempered to their barbarism. In fact, Calvin uses 'accommodation' and equivalent terms all over the place. A cynic might say that whenever the going gets tough Calvin plays the accommodation card, or more charitably, that he has recourse to the term as a sort of habit of mind.

So there is a sense in which for Calvin all language from God about himself and his ways – his revelation – must be accommodated to us, given the difference between the Creator and his creatures. For we can never know God as he knows himself. But he also contrasts accommodated with non-accommodated (or perhaps with less-accommodated) language. Here is a well-known passage on divine repentance taken from his treatment of providence.

What, then, is meant by the term repentance? The very same that is meant by other forms of expression, by which God is described to us humanly. Because our weakness cannot reach his height, any description which we receive of him must be lowered to our capacity in order to be intelligible. And the mode of lowering is to represent him not as he really is, but as we conceive of him. Though he is incapable of every feeling of perturbation, he declares that he is angry with the wicked. Wherefore, as when we hear that God is angry, we ought not to imagine that there is any emotion in him, but ought rather to consider the mode of speech accommodated to our sense, God is appearing to us like one inflamed and irritated whenever he exercises judgment, so we ought not to imagine anything more under the term repentance than a change of action, men being wont to testify their dissatisfaction by such a change . . . in the mean time, there is no inversion of his counsel or will, no change of his affection. What from eternity he had foreseen, approved, decreed, he prosecutes with unvarying uniformity, how sudden soever to the eye of man the variation may seem to be.[2]

Calvin here contrasts God repenting with God being 'beyond all disturbance of mind'. In drawing this contrast, he is clearly referring to an understanding of God that we may have that is prior to God's 'accommodations'. Yet there must also be a sense in which even this language is accommodated. Take, for example, the way Scripture identifies separate divine attributes such as mercy, and grace, and omniscience and omnipotence. In common with the tradition going back at least as far as Augustine, Calvin believes (as we shall see) that God is a simple essence, that is, he is neither divisible nor composed out of parts that are more 'basic' than he is. So to talk of God's essential characteristics as if God has many separate attributes must for Calvin also be accommodated language even though, as far as I know, he never makes this point explicitly.

However, the kind of language that Calvin usually refers to as 'accommodated' is the result of God's choice, the choice of grace, as he comes down to his people through the prophets and the apostles, lisping to them like a nurse to a small child and lastly (but supremely) coming to us in his incarnate Son.

TRUE WISDOM

Central to Calvin's task as a Reformer was an epistemological issue: where is religious authority located, and how is that authority to be accessed? In brief, Calvin's answer to the question is that the authority is not in the church, nor in Christian tradition, but in Holy Scripture alone. And this source of authoritative knowledge is to be accessed by the believer himself or herself, with the indispensable aid of the ministry of the word and sacraments, energised by the Holy Spirit. Later on we shall consider the tensions that inevitably arise in Calvin's thought between the individual believer and the institutions of church and state. But before that we must focus on the individual, which is where Calvin begins.

Calvin's answer to the issue of religious authority raises a number of epistemological questions; notably, how is Scripture, the sole authority in religious matters, to be identified? How is it to be understood? And what degree of belief in it is appropriate? Considering Calvin's answers to these questions will occupy us for the remainder of this chapter.

The opening sentences of the *Institutes*, sentences that appeared at the head of every edition of that great work, and particularly the first two sentences, are richly epistemological. 'Our wisdom, in so far as it ought to be deemed true and solid wisdom, consists almost entirely of two parts: the knowledge of God and of ourselves. But as these are connected together by many ties, it is not easy to determine which of the two precedes, and gives birth to the other'.[3] We must note certain features of what Calvin says here, as well as noting what he is not saying. First, the emphasis on *wisdom*. As we saw in Chapter 1, for Calvin the Christian religion offers a method of possessing true and sound wisdom, and this wisdom consists in a certain kind and range of knowledge. For Calvin wisdom is not a matter of gaining or inventing the correct method of acquiring facts, nor is it the enjoyment of as much error-free belief as we can achieve, but it lies in a particular kind of knowledge of God and of ourselves.

As we have also noted, Calvin taps into one mediaeval emphasis, that the Christian religion has to do with imparting *sapientia*, and he implicitly rejects another mediaeval emphasis, that theology has to do chiefly with theoretical understanding and certainty, *scientia*. In this sense Calvin is a Franciscan rather than a Dominican. Theology does not provide us merely with more knowledge in the form of more explanations, as nuclear physics and astronomy and criminal detection do, but with true wisdom. It has to do with the *knowledge* of God, certainly, but with that sort of knowledge that enables us to enjoy the favour and presence of God, and which will bring us to our everlasting home. For Calvin seizes every opportunity to contrast the sort of knowledge of God which 'flits in the brain', which he despises and which hardly counts as knowledge at all, and the knowledge (*notitia*) that promotes the love of God and willing obedience to him.

It is an exaggeration to say that for Calvin the knowledge of God is mere know-how, but there is nevertheless more than a grain of truth in this. Here is one place at least where the affinity of Calvin's thought is more with John Bunyan's *Pilgrim's Progress* than it is with Aquinas's *Summa Theologiae*. We must note too that Calvin's preferred term for what such knowledge confers was not *theologia* (a word which, after all, was the invention of Aristotle) but *religio*, the binding of the self to God.

This wisdom is to be found in the knowledge of God and of ourselves. Where did Calvin (and the tradition) get this emphasis on wisdom? One obvious answer is that he simply took it from Scripture, from its teaching Christ as the wisdom of God, from its warnings against the wisdom of this world, from the 'wisdom literature' and especially from the Psalms. But there are other possible sources, too, not incompatible with this. Suppose we ask, where does the emphasis on a twofold knowledge, of God and of ourselves, emerge from? It is one of the very many things that Calvin took from Augustine of Hippo. The supreme importance for Augustine of this twofold knowledge, of God and of ourselves, is found vividly in the *Confessions*. In his wonderful discussion of memory in Book X he says, addressing his Lord, 'to hear you speaking about oneself is to know oneself' and 'what I know of myself I know because you grant me light'.[4] The fundamental point is stated with deliberate plainness, and rather more formally, in the *Soliloquies,* 'I desire to know God and the soul. Nothing more? Nothing at all.'[5]

But although Calvin undoubtedly borrowed from Augustine, he gave this relation between the knowledge of God and of ourselves his own distinctive twist. But in any case, he did not *quite* say what Augustine said, did he? He did not add Augustine's 'nothing more'. There is evidence in the *Institutes* and elsewhere that there were other things that Calvin desired to know – other subordinate sources of wisdom than the self in its relation to God. For instance, he was particularly fascinated and impressed by astronomy. He greatly admired the gifts of God's 'common grace', as we shall see in more detail later on. He's very careful to state, in the opening sentences of the *Institutes*, that wisdom almost entirely consists of two parts – almost entirely, but not quite – the knowledge of God and of ourselves.

The theologian John R. Franke, coming from the Reformed tradition, begins his book *The Character of Theology* by quoting the words of Calvin from the beginning of the *Institutes* that I have quoted. And then he says,

> Calvin's observation continues to provide a helpful model for reflecting on the character of theology and suggests that we must always be attentive not only to the knowledge of God but also to the knowledge of ourselves as human beings if we hope to practice an approach to theology that leads to wisdom . . . This suggests that in the discipline of theology we must take account of the particular social and intellectual settings in which we engage in theological reflection and exploration.[6]

Then follows what is by now an all-too-familiar appeal for us to be post-modernists in theology. But in this invocation of Calvin, Franke reveals a radical misunderstanding. Calvin is not saying that when we do theology (which concerns the knowledge of God) we are to be aware of the social and cultural setting in which we, as human beings, are placed (the knowledge of ourselves). This is a point almost too obvious to be worth noting. After all, the opening words of Book One of the *Institutes* are preceded by an elaborate *apologia* for the Reformation addressed to King Francis I of France. In this sense Calvin was a contextual theologian par excellence. In any case, in sixteenth century Geneva, Calvin could hardly have been unaware of his cultural setting! Franke has missed Calvin's distinctive twist, even though he quotes the very words that express it.

Calvin's point is that the knowledge of God and of ourselves are *immediately reciprocal*. In knowing God we at once – automatically, inevitably – gain true knowledge of ourselves, and in knowing ourselves we are at once led to know God. There is, so to speak, no choice in the matter. It is not that there are two distinct subject matters, God and ourselves, which it is wise to bring into some kind of positive relationship. No, for Calvin the knowledge of the one inevitably leads to the knowledge of the other; the knowledge of the other leads inevitably to the knowledge of the first.

As we see how Calvin works this out in the first few paragraphs of the *Institutes* we need to bear in mind that this is a work prepared for the Christian community. In the crisis of the Reformation, Calvin is attempting to set forth the character of the Christian religion to those who already confess Christ. So what does he tell them? He reminds them that the knowledge of God and of ourselves are 'connected together by many ties', but that 'it is not easy to determine which of the two precedes, and gives birth to the other'. If a properly functioning Christian reflects upon himself then his thoughts turn immediately to the contemplation of God. For his 'endowments' are clearly not of his own creation. But then Calvin changes key. Our 'miserable ruin' especially 'compels us to turn our eyes upwards'.

Thus, our feeling of ignorance, vanity, want, weakness, in short, depravity and corruption, reminds us that in the Lord, and none but He, dwell the true light of wisdom, solid virtue, exuberant goodness . . . we cannot aspire to him in earnest until we have begun to be displeased with ourselves.

We have knowledge of our own powers, which shows, by an immediate inference, that we come from God. But we also have knowledge of ourselves as fallen and 'Every person, therefore, on coming to this knowledge of himself, is not only to seek God, but is also led as by the hand to find him.'[7]
So, the knowledge of ourselves, but especially of our fallenness, leads us to God.

In the same way, the knowledge of God leads us to a knowledge of ourselves. 'Man never attains to a true self-knowledge until he have previously contemplated the face of God, and come down after such contemplation to look into himself.' Our innate pride is such that unless we look to the Lord, the sole standard of righteousness, we shall not be convinced 'of our injustice, vileness, folly, and impurity'.[8] And this standard is now to be found fully set forth in Holy Scripture and nowhere else.

These are words from the opening sections of the *Institutes*, a sort of preface, and they provide the orientation of the entire work, the orientation of Calvin's theology, even though, as we have seen, he would not have liked that word 'theology' applied to himself. Alternatively, we could say that these words are fundamental to Calvin's *world view*. They establish a pattern that is basic to Calvin's *Institutes* and to his entire thought: just as Martin Luther spoke of the Law preceding the Gospel, so too Calvin, in rather different tones, says the same thing: true wisdom consists in the identification of a deep need for God and in identifying God-in-Christ as the only one capable of satisfying that need. We do not naturally have such knowledge. We acquire it, or receive it, from God himself. More on this later.

The motif, the knowledge of God and of ourselves, recurs in the opening page of Book II. Calvin tells us that the trouble is not with the precept 'know thyself' but with the philosophers who think that it is a recipe for us to discover what fine people we are. We are, by nature, inclined to admire ourselves. But this is not true knowledge but self-deceit. To start with, nothing we have is our own, however excellent, but is the gift of God himself. But secondly, when we recognise our status, 'our miserable condition since Adam's fall, all confidence and boasting are overthrown, we blush for shame, and feel truly humble.'[9]

So the knowledge that we are to seek is not that which flatters, in which we are credulous about the superiority of our gifts:

> General credit is given to the very foolish idea, that man is perfectly sufficient of himself for all the purposes of a good and happy life . . . Accordingly, in every age, he who is most forward in extolling the excellence of human nature, is received with the loudest applause . . . Whosoever, therefore, gives heed to those teachers who merely employ us in contemplating our good qualities, so far from making progress in self-knowledge, will be plunged into the most pernicious ignorance.[10]

However, Calvin is not denying that we have good traits, gifts of God. 'It is not the will of God, however, that we should forget the primeval dignity which he bestowed on our first parents.'

> But such meditation, so far from raising our spirits, rather casts them down, and makes us humble. For what is our original? One from which we have fallen. What the end of our creation? One from which we have altogether strayed, so that, weary of our miserable lot, we groan, and groaning sigh for a dignity now lost. When we say that man should see nothing in himself which can raise his spirits, our meaning is, that he possesses nothing on which he can proudly plume himself.[11]

How ought we to proceed?

> In considering the knowledge which man ought to have of himself, it seems proper to divine it thus, *first*, to consider the end for which he was created, and the qualities – by no means contemptible qualities – with which he was endued, thus urging him to meditate on divine worship, and the future life; and, *secondly*, to consider his faculties, or rather want of faculties – a want which, when perceived, will annihilate all his confidence, and cover him with confusion.[12]

SENSUS DIVINITATIS

Important as this emphasis on the twofold knowledge of God is, to gain a more rounded estimate of Calvin's views we must take some steps backwards. For although Calvin held that to gain such knowledge we are to rely on what God in his word tells us, he also believed that the human race was originally endowed with a *sensus divinitatis*, an innate sense of divinity which, to begin with, picks up a knowledge of God not from God's word but from his world.

> That there exists in the human mind, and indeed by natural instinct, some sense of Deity, we hold to be beyond dispute, since God himself, to prevent any man from pretending ignorance, has endued all men with some idea of his Godhead, the memory of which he constantly renews and occasionally enlarges, that all to a man, being aware that there is a God, and that he is their Maker, may be condemned by their own conscience when they neither worship him nor consecrate their lives to his service. Certainly, if there is any quarter where it might be supposed that God is unknown, the most likely for such an instance to exist is among the dullest tribes farthest removed from civilization. But, as a heathen tells us, there is no nation so barbarous, no race so brutish, as not to be imbued with the conviction that there is a God.[13]

Calvin claims that this sense of God is natural and universal, and that it expresses itself in an awareness of God and in commitment to him.

So the basic position is that all mankind were created in the image of God and are endowed with this *sensus* in virtue of their humanity. This endowment has not been wiped out by the Fall, but it continues to function, or rather to malfunction, in us all. The knowledge conveyed has two aspects: the knowledge of God, which then leads us to serve him.

This *sensus* is that by which all men are 'aware that there is a God, and that he is their Maker'.[14] These expressions confirm Calvin's relative lack of interest in the *Institutes* in natural theology in the form of discursive proofs of God's existence. The *sensus* provides the knowledge that there is a deity to everyone in a direct and immediate way. But the *sensus* is not a direct experience of God and certainly not an acquaintance with God's essence. Rather by it all men conceive (or perceive) *that there is a God*. They form that belief immediately and naturally, even though they may be mistaken about the character of God and so fall into idolatry.

Another aspect of the *sensus* conveys an awareness of certain obligations arising out of the knowledge of the fact that God is the source of all goodness. He is our Creator.

> My meaning is: we must be persuaded not only that as he once formed the world, so he sustains it by his boundless power, governs it by his wisdom, preserves it by his goodness, in particular, rules the human race with justice and judgment, bears with them in mercy, shields them by his protection; but also that not a particle of light, or wisdom, or justice, or power, or rectitude, or genuine truth, will anywhere be found, which does not flow from him, and of which he is not the cause.[15]

This is corroborated by Calvin's later claim that the knowledge of God is sufficient to convey a sense of obligation.[16] So the awareness that God is our Creator triggers beliefs and feelings of awe, gratitude and a sense of obligation to our benefactor.

This is the natural, the original endowment of the human race. But Calvin also goes on, in Chapter 4 of Book 1 of the *Institutes*, to claim that this knowledge of God is corrupted as a result of the Fall.

> But though experience testifies that a seed of religion is divinely sown in all, scarcely one in a hundred is found who cherishes it in his heart, and not one in whom it grows to maturity, so far is it from yielding fruit in its season. Moreover, while some lose themselves in superstitious observances, and others, of set purpose, wickedly revolt from God, the result is that, in regard to the true knowledge of him, all are so degenerate, that in no part of the world can genuine godliness be found.[17]

Calvin appeals to Cicero in articulating his view of the *sensus*. Cicero's *The Nature of the Gods* is one of the main ancient sources for what is known as the Argument from Universal Consent for the existence of God. 'The crux of the matter is known to all men everywhere. From their birth it is inscribed upon their minds that gods exist'.[18] Belief in God is universal, and it arises from a predisposition. It is 'proleptic' in that it anticipates the arrival of evidence that there is a god.

Calvin derived this language from the Stoics, but he took the idea itself from what the Apostle Paul wrote in the first two chapters of

his letter to the Romans. It is important to note
to Cicero not in order to borrow his argumen
from human consent, but to provide indeper
universality of the awareness of God and tl
Cicero provides empirical evidence that corrobore.
by Paul in Romans. There Paul writes of a universal knov..
God which, due to sin, is suppressed and denied but not entirely
eradicated (Romans 1. 18–22). God exists, and (Cicero shows) experience confirms that the recognition of divinity is universal.

As we've already noted, Calvin held that the human race is fallen,
and that this has the unfortunate consequence of causing the *sensus*
to malfunction. How are we to understand this? One possibility is
that Calvin thinks that all men and women retain a sense of the true
God in their religious subconscious, which they then suppress or
transmute into an animistic or polytheistic or deistic variant of that.
But there is no evidence that he thinks in this way: Calvin does not
employ the idea of levels of consciousness and say that although
men and women may profess to be polytheists, or animists, deep
down they are monotheists of the sort that Calvin himself was. For
Calvin sinfulness is not to be understood as a state of ignorance or
false-consciousness brought about by self-deception even though
self-deception is an aspect of sin. Rather the knowledge of the true
God is wilfully perverted into false beliefs, as at the same time the
true knowledge (in Calvin's sense) of God is lost.

However, sin does not entirely remove the knowledge of God
afforded by the *sensus*, otherwise people would not be responsible for
what they do. In support of this Calvin explicitly rejects Plato's view
that we sin only out of ignorance and he endorses Aristotle's view of
sin as intemperance, as knowingly and stubbornly, without regret,
persisting in choosing evil.[19]

THE WORD OF GOD

It is because the *sensus* is perverted through rebelliousness, and men
and women languish without a true knowledge of God, that they
need the Word of God. It discloses his mercy and salvation, which is
necessary if we are to return to God and enjoy his favour.

Calvin does not often use 'revelation' or 'reveal' in connection with
Scripture, but instead he employs a variety of expressions such as
'proclaims' or 'declares'[20] and refers to the Bible as 'oracles'. Calvin also

s such terms as 'reveal', 'manifest' and 'disclose' in a wider sense,
o refer to what God continuously discloses about himself in the
world at large. God places himself 'in our view, that we cannot open
our eyes without being compelled to behold him'.[21]

Yet he undoubtedly thinks of Scripture as a divine revelation, an
unveiling of God's salvific purposes for the race and God's remedial
revelation. In furthering his redemptive plan God discloses his nature
and his ways through prophets and apostles, and supremely in Christ.
We shall here focus on Calvin's understanding of the epistemology
of such disclosure, leaving what he says about the content of God's
revelation for later.

Calvin says that if we are to come to God, as distinct from having
merely hazy ideas of God drawn from our fallen nature, then we need
'the light of his Word'.[22] So God has supplemented 'those common
proofs by the addition of his Word, as a sure and more direct means
of discovering himself'.[23] For Calvin, doctrine is essential to religion,
and true doctrine, truth that is necessary and enough for our salvation, is to be found in Scripture. But how do we come to have this
conviction?

In setting out his understanding of revelation and of its epistemology, Calvin is in effect (as part of the Reformation conflict) asking
and answering the question of where ultimate religious authority is
located. His answer is the Bible, whose authority does not derive in
two steps from the endorsement of some higher human authority,
such as the Councils of the Church, or tradition, or the Papacy, but
in *one* step from God himself, for God manifests himself in Scripture.
We come to have the conviction that Scripture is God's Word from
Scripture itself. Scripture is logically prior to the church. In saying
that Scripture has this supremacy and finality, Calvin is not saying
that other sources have no value. Obviously not. But the Bible is not
one source among many others; it is the judge of all other sources.

This conviction that the knowledge of God may be acquired in
one step, not two, is at the core of what Calvin refers to as the self-
authenticating or self-witnessing character of Scripture.

> Let it therefore be held as fixed, that those who are inwardly taught
> by the Holy Spirit acquiesce implicitly in Scripture; that Scripture,
> carrying its own evidence along with it, deigns not to submit to
> proofs and arguments, but owes the full conviction with which we
> ought to receive it to the testimony of the Spirit. Enlightened by

him, we no longer believe, either on our own judgment or that of others, that the Scriptures are from God; but, in a way superior to human judgment, feel perfectly assured – as much so as if we beheld the divine image visibly impressed on it – that it came to us, by the instrumentality of men, from the very mouth of God.[24]

Self-authentication is a consequence or corollary of Calvin's emphasis that only God can witness to God and that only if God *directly* witnesses to himself is that witness thoroughly trustworthy. It is direct in that no distinct, intermediary human endorsement is necessary. This is why Calvin believes that he is warranted in using verbs such as 'witness', 'disclose' and 'speak'. How does the Spirit witness? Not by enabling us to exercise a leap of faith in Scripture (in the manner of Pascal or Kierkegaard, perhaps) but by powerfully disclosing to us the cognitive and affective content of Scripture, its 'message'. So Calvin's approach to Scripture is not fideistic. He holds that belief that Scripture as God's word ought to be based upon evidence that it is so. But this is supernaturally imbued evidentialism rather than a naturalistic evidentialism. The cognitive content of Scripture is objectively clear and true. It is not that it is vague, or ambiguous, and that the Holy Spirit helps us to 'make something' of it. Rather, confronted by this evidence, and having the assurance from the Spirit that this is the voice of God, we shall be utterly convinced that what Scripture tells us is the word of God himself.

Surprisingly, however, despite this emphasis on the internal work of the Spirit on the heart,[25] at this point in the *Institutes* Calvin also provides a sympathetic treatment of what he calls 'proofs' or 'helps' in confirming our belief.[26] Nevertheless, Calvin intends that these 'external' proofs play a subordinate role to the appeal to the self-authenticating character of Scripture. So the basic one-step approach to recognising Scripture's divine authority makes possible this two-step appeal to the trustworthiness of Scripture through the attention we may give to the external evidence that Scripture is a unique library of books.

In making this distinction between internal and external proofs, and in the relative value which he places on each, Calvin shows himself to be in line with the mediaeval treatment of God's special revelation.[27]

What is the point of the 'external proofs', then? They are 'aids' in fortifying the authority of Scripture by arguments.[28] But not all these data are 'external' to Scripture. Among them is Scripture's truthfulness as seen in the frankness of the writers, who often testify against themselves to their own disadvantage. Calvin treats Moses as something of a paradigm; just as Moses' own word was confirmed by publicly witnessed miracles, so is Scripture more generally. Prophecies prove their genuineness by being against expectations. Scripture has been preserved down the centuries. The style of the evangelists, and Paul's remarkable conversion, testify to the genuineness and authority of the New Testament. Such data, Calvin thinks, offer cumulative evidence attesting the credibility of Scripture.

What is the epistemic value of these various appeals, which Calvin says is a mere selection of the many others that could be given? He believes that they confirm the truth of Scripture and 'vindicate' it against its disparagers. They form part of an apologetic strategy of a 'negative' kind, not establishing the authority of Scripture but rebutting objections to it. Even considered cumulatively, such 'proofs' are insufficient to produce faith

> until our heavenly Father manifest his presence in it, and thereby secure implicit reverence for it. Then only, therefore, does Scripture suffice to give a saving knowledge of God when its certainty is founded on the inward persuasion of the Holy Spirit . . . But it is foolish to attempt to prove to infidels that the Scripture is the Word of God. This cannot be known to be, except by faith.[29]

Why does Calvin regard these proofs as 'external'? Because they abstract from the distinctive content of Scripture, its 'message', and so in this sense their authority can only be subsidiary.

For Calvin the heart of the matter is that Scripture itself testifies its divine authority through what it tells us about God and about ourselves. It is the Holy Spirit who causes the divinely authored Word and therefore the authority of Scripture – that authority which it has inherently – to shine in the hearts and minds of believers. The Spirit does not produce the authority, he witnesses to it. Calvin sees the production of this recognition of authority in strongly personal terms. It is the result of the activity of God the Holy Spirit on the soul, and it is an integral part of God's redemptive grace to sinners. This is something which the mediaevals did not so much deny as largely ignored, but which he brings to the forefront and stresses. Freed from the sacramentalism of the mediaeval outlook, Calvin lays special emphasis on the work of God's Holy Spirit by and through his Word.

> If, then, we would consult most effectually for our consciences, and save them from being driven about in a whirl of uncertainty, from wavering, and even stumbling at the smallest obstacle, our conviction of the truth of Scripture must be derived from a higher source than human conjectures, judgments or reasons; namely, the secret testimony of the Spirit.[30]

Calvin is not here saying that the activity of the Spirit which is sufficient to establish the authority of the Word of God is unreasonable or irrational or non-rational in character. How could that be when the Spirit is the Spirit of the most wise and all-knowing God? 'Scripture is its own evidence' means what it says. The Spirit's work is not a purely subjective persuasion, a groundless feeling of conviction. It is rather that the Spirit testifies to or illumines the cognitive content of the objectively true Scripture. Strictly speaking, such illumination does not need any rational or empirical considerations external to the message of Scripture to add further support to it even though such data may be provided.

In Calvin's employment of both internal and external proofs of this fundamental feature of his theology, we must note the tension between what we may call the 'orderly' versus the 'disorderly' aspects of Calvin's thought. Appealing to the external proofs is 'orderly': such 'proofs' can be studied, taught and argued about. By the use of them in preaching and teaching the authority of Scripture can be safeguarded in the churches. By contrast the internal testimony of the Holy Spirit to the Word is 'disorderly', or at least potentially so; it is granted personally, at the behest of the Spirit who is, as Calvin stresses, sovereign in dispensing this gift. Such a gift and its reception cannot be built into the educational and political structures of the church: it cannot be bequeathed by the church's ministry to the next generation in any way that guarantees success. Here is an area of tension in Calvin's thought that we shall encounter again and have more to say about.

Calvin brackets together self-authentication and certainty, and he contrasts (in terms of certainty) the self-authentication of Scripture (which, he says, is 'perfectly assured')[31] and the external proof of Scripture (which, he says, is a matter of opinion). For Calvin there appears to be necessary connection between a self-authenticating experience of something and the utter certainty of the presence or the truth of that thing.

By knowledge we do not mean comprehension, such as that which we have of things falling under human sense. For that knowledge is so much superior, that the human mind must far surpass and go beyond itself in order to reach it. Nor even when it has reached it does it comprehend what it feels, but persuaded of what it comprehends not, it understands more from mere certainty of persuasion than it could discern of any human matter by its own capacity.[32]

On Calvin's view the sources of the knowledge of God have a practical function; God's revelation is more like a handbook or recipe book than a theoretical treatise. So when Calvin says of the certainty of faith that the certainty it requires must be full and decisive, 'as is usual in regard to matters ascertained and proved',[33] he might seem to be arguing that such certainty is not superior to certainty about mundane matters, but is in the same class, and that it has to be understood by reference to the sort of certainty which obtains in such cases.

So Calvin insists that the Bible authenticates itself by evidencing itself to us through the work of the Holy Spirit. He does not refer to 'self-evidence' (as this term is used in modern epistemology) in this connection, nor even to 'evidence', but uses equivalents such as 'manifest signs'. Yet it is clear, from the structure of Calvin's discussion in *Institutes* I.6–9, that he is all the time eager to focus on the content of Scripture. It is this content, its redemptive-historical 'message', that manifests itself and not Scripture considered formally as a library of 66 books each of which share certain distinguishing features. We have already seen that he thinks that 'external' proofs have limited value. In addition, he is scathing in his denunciation of the left wing of the Reformation, (the 'radical Reformation'), the 'Libertines' as he calls them, who insist upon separating the Spirit from the Word.

The firm belief in the divinity of the Scriptures is formed by accepting evidence which the Scripture itself presents; the person thus convinced has the belief on the basis of that evidence. The internal testimony of the Holy Spirit makes available to the minds of men and women, the objective grounds, the *indicia*, internal to Scripture itself, and the acceptance of these grounds is what provides the evidence of its being God's Word. The Spirit does this by so presenting that evidence that according to Calvin the belief is held (ideally, as we have seen) with utter certainty.

But forming the conviction in this way that the Bible is the revelation of God himself is not an isolated occurrence. It is not a *prolegomenon* that is detachable from other aspects of the Christian life. To be faithful to Calvin's thrust, the Spirit's witness to the authority of Scripture must be seen as one aspect, no doubt a fundamental aspect, of the entire life of faith. For Calvin faith has to do with the promises of God, and the promises of God are to found only in Scripture. He would no doubt concede that the ups and downs of faith, which he later discusses in the *Institutes*,[34] may also be reflected in the believer's strength of conviction that the Bible is God's Word. That conviction also may have its ups and downs. Faith is the gift of the Holy Spirit, and one aspect of such faith is trust in God, and such trust can fluctuate, as convictions about the meaning and truth of Scripture ebb and flow. Nevertheless, faith at its best is a form of knowledge, but not knowledge of the sort that can be demonstrated.

As he draws his discussion of Scripture and faith (in Book I of the *Institutes*) to a close, Calvin writes 'I do not dwell on this subject at present, because we will return to it again; only let us now understand that the only true faith is that which the Spirit of God seals on our hearts.'[35] He resumes his discussion of faith at the beginning of Book III. We shall return to these themes in Chapter 5.

CHAPTER 3

GOD IN TRINITY

We turn from considering how according to Calvin we may have reliable information about God to consider what God has revealed to us about himself. As we have noted, `Calvin draws a fundamental distinction between God *in se* (as he is in himself) and God *quoad nos* (as he is revealed to us). The wisdom of God that we have the benefit of is what he has been pleased to disclose to us about himself, especially regarding his salvific purposes. Who God is as he is in himself is a matter of profitless speculation and a misguided effort to transcend the Creator-creature distinction.

This distinction between God as he is and God as he reveals himself to us applies to all of Calvin's discussions of God. So in his deliberations about the Trinity, while God is in himself Trinitarian, Calvin is most concerned with God's Trinitarian character as this is revealed in what he does for us. The distinction is not a novel one. For example, Aquinas offers illuminating precedents for it, even if he is not the direct intellectual source of them.[1] But perhaps the consequences of this distinction are of more importance for Calvin than for many of his predecessors.

God's essence – God himself – is simple and incomprehensible, 'simple and undivided'.[2]

> When we profess to believe in one God, by the name God is understood the one simple essence, comprehending three persons or hypostases; and accordingly, whenever the name of God is used indefinitely, the Son and Spirit, not less than the Father, is meant. But when the Son is joined with the Father, relation comes into view, and so we distinguish between the Persons.[3]

Note that while Calvin asserts God's incomprehensibility, in the same breath he claims that in God we 'comprehend' three persons. For Calvin, to say that God is incomprehensible is not to say that all our talk about him is gibberish or incoherent. He means, more exactly, that our minds, creaturely minds, cannot encompass the divine nature. Nevertheless, we can know something of God; we can *apprehend* him; otherwise divine revelation to us would be impossible. This distinction needs to be kept in mind in what follows.

Calvin is an eternalist; that is, he holds that God exists beyond or outside time. Perhaps the idea of divine simplicity entails eternalism, although he does not say as much. Nonetheless, he clearly affirms both positions.

> When we attribute prescience to God, we mean that all things always were, and ever continue, under his eye; that to his knowledge there is no past or future, but all things are present, and indeed so present, that it is not merely the idea of them that is before him (as those objects are which we retain in our memory), but that he truly sees and contemplates them as actually under his immediate inspection. This prescience extends to the whole circuit of the world, and to all creatures.[4]

Calvin believes that while we cannot comprehend God's essence nonetheless God reveals something of it to us, what Calvin refers to as his *nature*. The two are distinct but connected. God's activities, according to Calvin, partly reveal his nature and they are, in turn, partial and adapted expressions of his essence and, so to speak, endorsed or guaranteed by it.

> He [the Psalmist] does not speak of the hidden and mysterious essence of God which fills heaven and earth, but of the manifestations of his power, wisdom, goodness, and righteousness, which are clearly exhibited, although they are too vast for our limited understanding to comprehend.[5]

Paradoxically, while it is the simplicity of God's essence that makes it incomprehensible to us at the same time God's essence guarantees his immutability. God's *essence* is what he is. His *nature* is what of his essence God has revealed to us in a way or ways that we can grasp.

So while God alone knows himself, his own essence, immediately and directly, by God's gracious revelation we may know God's nature and thereby apprehend aspects of his essence. This revelation is indirect, in the form of sets of assertions or propositions about God's words and actions. Because the nature and the essence of God are connected insofar as the first partly reveals the second, we know that faithfulness is part of God's essence (part of what God is). Even though we cannot perceive or fully comprehend that essence, we can say (on the basis of what God has revealed to us about himself) that it is impossible for God to fail to be faithful (to fail to be what he is). So if God freely decrees this or that, his freedom is always a freedom exercisable only in accordance with his immutable essence, though it would be perverse to regard this as a 'limitation' upon God. God is not capricious or lawless, therefore.

God's nature (as distinct from his essence), then, is expressed and summed up in what he is towards us. His nature is revealed in what God has freely chosen to do. These activities express God's nature directly – for example, in the wisdom and righteousness that they display – but they express his essence only obliquely.

If we could break up the divine essence so as to be able to consider, say, divine power apart from divine justice, then it would be possible to speculate about what a God who was all-powerful but not just might command or perform. But Calvin will not countenance this. He abhors any thinking about God that separates and plays off one of his features against the others. We must hold together in fact what appears to be separable in thought. This is another way in which, according to Calvin, our knowledge that God has an immutable though incomprehensible essence must control all our thinking and speaking about him.

We can make distinctions about God – between his various attributes – and in particular between the persons of the Trinity, but these *distinctions* do not correspond to *divisions* in God. Presumably Calvin's reasoning here goes (or would go) like this: only what has parts is divisible; God is without parts; therefore, God is indivisible. Even if we can distinguish between God's wisdom and his power, these are characteristics of one and the same God, just as distinguishing between Father, Son and Spirit does not imply that there are three gods or three parts to God.

While for Calvin God's simple essence is not a black hole, it is nevertheless best approached in a guarded, rather negative way. We speak most sensibly about God's essence when we say what it is not (e.g. God is not changeable, is not in time) and when we exercise reserve and restraint in our positive statements. And we may also say that for Calvin, as for the entire tradition that accepts the idea of divine simplicity, God is incomprehensible to us partly at least *because* he is simple.

Exodus 34.6 is fundamental for Calvin, as for others. Calvin's comments in the *Institutes* on this passage show us his fundamental approach to God's revealed nature.

Here we may observe, *first*, that his eternity and self-existence are declared by his magnificent name twice repeated; and, *secondly*, that in the enumeration of his perfections, he is described not as he is in himself, but in relation to us, in order that acknowledgement of him may be more a vivid actual impression than empty visionary speculation. Moreover, the perfections thus enumerated are just those which we saw shining in the heavens, and on the earth – compassion, goodness, mercy, justice, judgment and truth.[6]

Each of God's 'powers', his kindness, justice and so forth are rooted in his eternity and self-existence. We must constantly keep these divine attributes in mind if we are to understand properly everything else that God reveals to us about himself.

So Calvin knows *that* God is eternal, self-existent and all-good, but he does not know *what* God is; he does not comprehend the divine essence of which eternity, self-existence and complete goodness are aspects. Only God knows, in this comprehensive, immediate sense, what God is. Yet the fact that we know that God is eternal, self-existing and all-good and that these are features of his essence does a great deal of theological and religious work for Calvin. Reference to God's essence – even though that essence is incomprehensible to us – controls, in a kind of operational way, our understanding of and our attitude to God as he is to us.[7]

Likewise, God's revealed majesty and glory is inseparable from his essence.

The majesty, or the authority, or the glory of God does not consist in some imaginary brightness, but in those works which so necessarily belong to him, that they cannot be separated from his very essence. It is what peculiarly belongs to God, to govern the world, and to exercise care over mankind, and also to make a difference between good and evil, to help the miserable, to punish all wickedness, to check injustice and violence. When any one takes away these things from God, he leaves him an idol only.[8]

Calvin's repeated references to God's incomprehensible essence are also intended to warn us against imagining what God is like, which would lead us inexorably down the road to idolatry. Recognising God's infinite and spiritual essence keeps us from thinking that God can be represented in visual imagery. Calvin distinguishes between pictorial or iconic and verbal imagery. Visual representations of God would flout the Second Commandment. But Scripture abounds in figurative language about God, because in it God accommodates himself to us.

For who is so devoid of intellect as not to understand that God, in so speaking, lisps with us as nurses are wont to do with little children? Such modes of expression, therefore, do not so much express what kind of a being God is, as accommodate the knowledge of him to our feebleness. In doing so, he must, of course, stoop far below his proper height.[9]

So the contrast between God as he is in himself and as he is towards us is warranted both by the fact of God's incomprehensible essence and by the voluntariness of his creative and redemptive activities. As these activities arise from God's free choice, they do not and cannot fully reveal God as he is in himself, even if we were in a position to comprehend him in that way. This is not because God's activities are arbitrary but because they are contingent and so do not afford exhaustive accounts of his essence.

Here, if anywhere, in considering the hidden mysteries of Scripture, we should speculate soberly and with great moderation, cautiously guarding against allowing either our mind or our tongue to go a step beyond the confines of God's word. For how can the human mind, which has not yet been able to ascertain of what the body of the sun consists, though it is daily presented to the eye, bring down the boundless essence of God to its little measure? Nay, how can it, under its own guidance, penetrate to a knowledge of the substance of God while unable to understand its own? Wherefore, let

us willingly leave to God the knowledge of himself. In the words
of Hilary (De Trinit. lib.1), 'He alone is a fit witness to himself
who is known only by himself.' This knowledge, then, if we would
leave to God, we must conceive of him as he has made himself
known, and in our inquiries make application to no other quarter
than his word.[10]

CALVIN'S RESTRAINED TRINITARIANISM

Writing of the 'order' of the persons in the Trinity, Calvin says:

> Moreover, though the eternity of the Father is also the eternity
> of the Son and Spirit, since God never could be without his own
> wisdom and energy; and though in eternity there can be no room
> for first or last, still the distinction of order is not unmeaning or
> superfluous, the Father being considered first, next the Son from
> him, and then the Spirit from both.[11]

Although Calvin gives primary attention to Scripture's teaching
on God's Trinitarian character, as we noted in Chapter 1 he is not a
flat-footed biblicist. He thinks it is permissible, and even necessary,
to use language and concepts drawn from extra-biblical sources to
articulate – and in particular to defend – the biblical doctrine.

There is a tension here between, on the one hand, Calvin's commitment to the divine spirituality and immensity and to divine simplicity
and atemporalism (which induce in him a reserve in his theological
approach to God in himself) and, on the other hand, the explicitly
Trinitarian declarations of the New Testament. Addressing this tension, Calvin warmly endorses the approach of Hilary of Poitiers
and of Augustine in their use of terms such as *person* and *substance*
in characterising the Trinity, even though Scripture does not do so.
At the same time he endorses the reticence of the Fathers about
pressing the meaning of these terms. He refers approvingly to this
passage from Hilary:

> The guilt of the heretics and blasphemers compels us to undertake
> what is unlawful, to scale arduous heights, to speak of the ineffa-
> ble, and to trespass upon forbidden places. And since by faith
> alone we should fulfill what is commanded, namely, to adore the

Father, to venerate the Son with Him, and to abound in the Holy Spirit, we are forced to raise our lowly words to subjects that cannot be described. By the guilt of another we are forced into guilt, so that what should have been restricted to the pious contemplation of our minds is now exposed to the dangers of human speech.[12]

Augustine held that 'from the poverty of human language in so high a matter: not that the reality could be thereby expressed, (i.e. by the term 'hypostasis'), but that he might not pass on in silence without attempting to show how the Father, Son and Spirit are three.'[13] He went on to say, in the passage which Calvin quotes,

> For the sake, then, of speaking of things that cannot be uttered, that we may be able in some way to utter what we are able in no way to utter fully, our Greek friends have spoken of one essence, three substances; but the Latins of one essence or substance, three persons; because, as we have already said, essence usually means nothing else than substance in our language, that is, in Latin. And provided that what is said is understood only in a mystery, such a way of speaking was sufficient, in order that there might be something to say when it was asked what the three are, which the true faith pronounces to be three, when it both declares that the Father is not the Son, and that the Holy Spirit, which is the gift of God, is neither the Father nor the Son.[14]

Augustine's point is that the word 'person' when used of the Father, Son and Spirit warrants certain kinds of thought and speech about God. When the New Testament refers to God the Son we are warranted in treating the Son as one who is a subject of a certain range of predicates, some of which he has in common with the Father (his divinity) and others distinct from the other two persons of the godhead (his Sonship). What distinguish the persons, then, are certain relational predicates each of which expresses a 'peculiar subsistence.'[15]

Father, Son and Spirit are three 'who's', three 'someones or other' about whom we can and must say different things. The language of three 'persons' allows us to say that there are properties possessed by the Son that are not possessed by the Father and vice versa, a position surely endorsed by the New Testament. But it would be a mistake to think that the three 'persons' of the Trinity are like three distinct human beings with a common human nature. To think that would be to hold that God is divided into three. What would then stop us from thinking of the three divine persons as three gods? So the term 'person' is to be used with self-awareness and some care.

In Calvin's view, then, the use of one kind of expression for God's threeness ('person') and another kind of expression for God's oneness ('nature' or 'essence' or 'substance') safeguards New Testament language about the trinity of the Father, the Son and the Holy Spirit. Such usage not only keeps us from manifest inconsistency but also guides us into thinking and saying the right kinds of thing in turn about God the Father, about God the Son and about God the Spirit.

Calvin's endorsement of the use of the terms 'person', 'substance' and 'Trinity' in Christian thinking about the godhead, along with his warnings elsewhere about the introduction of extra-biblical terms such as 'merit', reveals some tension in his overall attitude to extra-biblical language. It is not easy to find any place where he discusses his view in a way that provides us with an overall, consistent picture of it. On the one hand, he believes that some extra-biblical language is permissible – and even required – to identify and exclude heretical teaching. On the other hand, he hesitates to endorse models or analogies that attempt to explain the Trinitarian mystery or God's providence. For instance, in an obvious allusion to Augustine's analogies in *On the Trinity*, Calvin says,

> I am not sure whether it is expedient to borrow analogies from human affairs to express the nature of this distinction. The ancient fathers sometimes do so, but they at the same time admit that what they bring forward as analogous is very widely different. And hence it is that I have a great dread of anything like presumption here, lest some rash saying may furnish an occasion of calumny to the malicious, or of delusion to the unlearned.[16]

Yet Calvin himself does not always shrink from such rashness. He readily appeals to the relation between mind and body as an analogy of Christ's divine and human nature, as we shall see in Chapter 4. Yet when he debates the nature of divine providence he is opposed on principle to the use of analogies of divine activity drawn from human affairs and not from Scripture. Calvin's general reluctance to use analogies drawn from outside Scripture, to indulge in 'thought experiments', underlines his anti-speculative temper. Overall, he is somewhat ambivalent about the use of analogies to aid theological understanding. Calvin's restraint over the Trinity is seen in another, rather surprising, way. He says,

> Where names have not been invented rashly, we must beware lest we become chargeable with arrogance and rashness in rejecting them. I wish, indeed, that such names were buried, provided all would concur in the belief that the Father, Son, and Spirit, are one God, and yet that the Son is not the Father, nor the Spirit the Son, but that each has his peculiar subsistence.[17]

Although Calvin always believed it was necessary to go beyond the very words of Scripture in order to elucidate the doctrine of the Trinity, it seems that were it not for the controversy about the Trinity that recurrently plagued him he would have been content to express the doctrine in that very simple form of words. The formula is an emphatic endorsement of the full deity of the three persons, and (perhaps because of this) it contains nothing, however hallowed by usage, that might serve to diminish this emphasis. So Calvin is here silent on the claim that the Son is begotten of the Father or that the Holy Spirit proceeds from the Father and the Son. It seems that he would prefer to leave such claims to one side by neither affirming them nor denying them.

Calvin offers a minimalist expression of the Trinity in order to avoid speculation or extravagance of some other kind that might ultimately prove to harbour heresy. In particular, he was emphatic on the full and undiminished deity of the Son. So despite his willingness to use non-biblical terminology he favours a formulation of the doctrine of the Trinity that uses neither 'Trinity', nor 'person' nor 'substance', nor the begetting of the Son nor the procession of the Spirit.

DID CALVIN'S VIEW OF THE TRINITY DEVELOP?

Yet Calvin's increased awareness of the subtleties of Arianism, particularly during his notorious controversy with Michael Servetus from 1546 onwards, forced him to go beyond this minimum, as did other controversies: with his fellow countryman Pierre Caroli in 1537, and later on, from 1558, that with Valentin Gentile and Giorgio Blandrata, both of whom were members of the Italian congregation in Geneva.[18] These debates made it necessary for him to be more explicit in his Trinitarianism, and this becomes more apparent in the succeeding editions of the *Institutes* in which the results of such controversies were added. As in this passage,

> The Father certainly cannot differ from the Son, unless he have something peculiar to himself, and not common to him with the Son. What, then, do these men show as the mark of distinction? If it is in the essence, let them tell whether or not he communicated essence to the Son. This he could not do in part merely, for it were impious to think of a divided God. And besides, on this supposition, there would be a rending of the Divine essence. The whole entire essence must therefore be common to the Father and the Son; and if so, in respect of essence there is no distinction between them.[19]

Since God is one simple essence, the distinctions between the persons of the Trinity cannot be sought in a dividing up of that essence. The distinctions must be expressed differently, and Calvin falls back on Augustine in emphasising that while each person is wholly and perfectly God, each is in unique relations to the others.

> For though we admit that, in respect of order and gradation, the beginning of divinity is in the Father, we hold it a detestable fiction to maintain that essence is proper to the Father alone, as if he were the deifier of the Son. On this view either the essence is manifold, or Christ is God only in name and imagination. If they grant that the Son is God, but only in subordination to the Father, the essence which in the Father is unformed and unbegotten will in him be formed and begotten.[20]

It is this idea, that the Father is the 'deifier' of the Son, that led to an incident that became notorious. When called upon by Caroli to endorse the Nicene and Athanasian creeds Calvin refused to do so. 'We have professed faith in God alone, not in Athanasius, whose Creed has not been approved by any properly constituted Church'.[21] Here is, in B. B. Warfield's words, Calvin's 'constant and firm determination to preserve full liberty to deal with the doctrine [viz. of the Sonship of God] free from all dictation from without or even prescription of traditional modes of statement'.[22] Throughout these debates Calvin was adamant about rejecting language that suggests a subordination of the divinity of the Son to the divinity of the Father and so might be thought to compromise it. Part of his unwillingness to confess his Trinitarianism in the very language of the Nicene Creed was due to its battology, 'God from God, Light from Light, true God from true God', because, he said, 'it adds neither to the emphasis nor to the expressiveness of the document'.[23] Calvin thought the language was more like a chant than a creed.

Given his generally conservative spirit, his refusal to be bound by the Nicene language looks awkward. We must put it down to his strong conviction that the Son is unqualifiedly God himself. Nevertheless, he endorses the idea of the eternal begottenness of the *person* of the Son at various places,[24] and so he does not so much offer a fundamental critique of the language of subordinationism as understand the subordination to concern the *person* rather than the *deity* of the Son. His basic conviction remains that each person of the Trinity is God himself and so exists *a se*.

On the other hand, the Scriptures demonstrate that there is some distinction between the Father and the Word, the Word and the Spirit; but the magnitude of the mystery reminds us of the great reverence and soberness which ought to be employed in discussing it. It seems to me, that nothing can be more admirable than the words of Gregory Nazianzen. 'I cannot think of the unity without being irradiated by the Trinity: I cannot distinguish between the Trinity without being carried up to the unity'. Therefore, let us beware of imagining such a Trinity of persons as will distract our thoughts, instead of bringing them instantly back to the unity.[25]

But as the Personal subsistencies carry an order with them, the principle and origin being in the Father, whenever mention is made of the Father and Son, or of the Father and Spirit together, the name of God is specially given to the Father. In this way the unity of essence is retained, and respect is had to the order, which, however, derogates in no respect from the divinity of the Son and Spirit.[26]

As regards the Son, Calvin's discussion of the nature of Christ's Sonship in the 1559 edition of the *Institutes* is clearly influenced by his controversy during 1556–7 over the antitrinitarian views of Gentile, a dispute that culminated in Gentile's trial in 1558. But his general concern over what he regarded as perverse misinterpretations of the doctrine of the Trinity antedates this controversy. It is found, for example, in the 1536 edition of the *Institutes*.[27]

In his general approach to the Trinity, Calvin is establishing certain non-negotiables. He emphasises the full deity and equality of each of the persons while at the same time assigning a primacy to the *person* of the Father from whom the Son in turn derives his own person. Calvin's thought, clarified and sharpened by the exchanges that we have mentioned, is that the language of subordinationism may be used provided it relates to the *personhood* of the Son and not to his essential deity, while modes of thought about the inter-Trinitarian relations that encourage or are the result of speculation ought to be avoided.

> In each hypostasis the whole nature is understood, the only difference being that each has his own peculiar subsistence. The whole Father is in the Son, and the whole Son in the Father . . . nor do ecclesiastical writers admit that the one is separated from the other by any difference of essence. 'By those names which denote distinction', says Augustine, 'is meant the relation which they mutually bear to each other, not the very substance by which they are one'. In this way, the sentiments of the Fathers, which might sometimes appear to be at variance with each other, are to be reconciled . . . Therefore, when we speak of the Son simply, without reference to the Father, we truly and properly affirm that he is of himself, and, accordingly, call him the only beginning; but when we note the relation which he bears to the Father, we correctly make the Father the beginning of the Son.[28]

Even in this more nuanced discussion of the Trinity, Calvin pays much less attention to the procession of the Spirit from the Father and the Son. But he does not deny it, upholding the *filioque* clause.

> So then it is Christ who sends the Spirit, but it is from the heavenly glory, that we may know that it is not a gift of men, but a sure pledge of Divine grace. Hence it appears how idle was the subtlety of the Greeks, when they argued, on the ground of these words, that the Spirit does not *proceed* from the Son; for here Christ,

according to his custom, mentions *the Father*, in order to raise our eyes to the contemplation of his Divinity.[29]

Note that Calvin here relies on a text that involves the economic arrangements within the Trinity to warrant belief in the Spirit's immanent relation to Father and Son. In the *Institutes*, he strongly affirms the Spirit's divinity,[30] and includes the Spirit in his discussion on sameness and difference among the persons of the Trinity. This discussion includes brief remarks on the relation of the Spirit to the Father and the Son. But when it is measured against the distinctive language of the Nicene formulation, Calvin's language is muted. Both the Son and the Spirit are said to 'come forth',[31] the former from the Father, the latter from the Father and the Son. Calvin uses this relation to enforce the 'simple unity' of God by noting that the Spirit is shared by the Father and the Son. Calvin eschews the subtleties involved in attempting to make clear the distinction between 'eternal begottenness' and 'eternal procession'.

THE ECONOMIC TRINITY

We turn finally to the question of how Calvin understood the relation between the persons of the Trinity as this is revealed in redemption and how therefore the economic Trinity and the immanent Trinity are related. The understanding of the Trinity that we have been outlining is only a necessary prelude to his development of the economic Trinity. For it is only the Triune God in his salvific operations, God as he is to us, who provides us with that knowledge of God which is not an 'bare and empty name' that 'flutters in our brain'.[32]

Calvin's conception of redemption is wholly and deeply Trinitarian. This follows from his resolute anti-subordinationism. The Son, being God himself, underivedly so, is a full participant in the 'devising' of human redemption. He is not a mere executor of the Father's will, as Karl Barth appears to have thought was Calvin's view,[33] but he is himself every bit as much the initiator or agent of redemption as is the Father. The same point applies to the person and the work of the Holy Spirit, though there is less emphasis on this in Calvin, perhaps because the issue was not controverted in his time.

One of Calvin's distinctive theological contributions is a rich and theologically central understanding of the Holy Spirit as Christ's Spirit. Not only in the matter of the authentication of Scripture, as we have already seen, but (together with Christ, Word of God) in promoting true spirituality, through the believer's union with Christ, and in 'realising' the ascended Christ's presence to worthy recipients in Baptism and the Supper. We shall look at both the idea of union with Christ and Calvin's understanding of the 'real presence' of Christ at the Supper, in later chapters.

So while the Son took on human nature this was not merely at the behest of the Father, nor at his own initiative, but in a way that reveals that he shares the initiative regarding human salvation with the Father. His taking on of human nature involves the Son's subordination to the word and will of the Father, as is clear in the New Testament (Jn. 4. 34, 6.38), but it is not only subordination, not merely the work of an executor. Rather the Son is, so to speak, a full member of the board. Calvin scorns those who 'insist that Christ was only the instrument or minister, not the author or leader, or prince of life, as he is designated by Peter [Acts. 3.15]'.[34] This is supported by the following quotation from Calvin's *Commentary* on Hebrews 1.3.

> When, therefore, thou hearest that the Son is the brightness of the Father's glory, think thus with thyself, that the glory of the Father is invisible until it shines forth in Christ, and that he is called the impress of his substance, because the majesty of the Father is hidden until it shews itself impressed as it were on his image.[35]

Calvin asserts the closest possible concurrence between the Father and the Son in the work of our redemption, as when he says:

> But, as many as were at last incorporated into the body of Christ were God's sheep, as Christ Himself testifies (Jn. 10.16), though formerly wandering sheep and outside the fold. Meantime, though they did not know it, the shepherd knew them, according to that eternal predestination by which He chose His own before the foundation of the world, as Augustine rightly declares.[36]

So who is the agent, or to use Barth's term, the 'Subject' of predestination, according to Calvin here? Not the Father, or at least not the Father apart from the Son. The Son himself, the shepherd, chose his own before the foundation of the world. He is the agent of election; he eternally chose his people and as a good shepherd laid down his life for them. But not in a way which separates him from the Father.

There is also another thought here, less familiar to us, perhaps. It appears that for Calvin the Mediatorship of the Son reaches more deeply than its vital place in human redemption. For Calvin holds – in one of his own pieces of speculation, surely – that 'had man remained free from all taint, he was of too humble a condition to penetrate to God without a Mediator'.[37] So the Son would have been the Mediator of the unfallen human race, as he is presently the Mediator between God and the unfallen angelic realm.[38] For Calvin 'Mediatorship' is a term with a cosmic reference, one that is not confined to human salvation. Nonetheless, it is a Mediatorship not merely assigned to the Son and willingly undertaken by him but also initiated by him. How could he fail to initiate it, since he is unqualifiedly *autotheos*, God himself?

It was his to swallow up death: who but Life could do so? It was his to conquer sin: who could do so save Righteousness itself? It was his to put to flight the powers of the air and the world: who could do so but the mighty power superior to both? But who possesses life and righteousness, and the dominion and government of heaven, but God alone? Therefore God, in his infinite mercy, having determined to redeem us, became himself our Redeemer in the person of his only-begotten Son.[39]

So what does all this tell us about how Calvin understood the relation between the economic and the immanent Trinity? Karl Rahner's so-called 'rule' states that 'The economic Trinity is the immanent Trinity and the immanent Trinity is the economic Trinity.'[40] This can be understood in several ways. Rahner may simply be reminding us that in referring to the 'economic Trinity' and the 'immanent Trinity' we are not referring to two Trinities but to only one. It is hard to imagine any Christian theologian dissenting from this, certainly not Calvin. Second, he may be expressing in a rather pointed way that it is only possible to *identify* the immanent Trinity through what is revealed about the economic Trinity. Or again, and more controversially, Rahner may be claiming a unity or identity in the sense that the economic Trinity is the only way in which the immanent Trinity *could* reveal itself. It is not clear that Calvin would subscribe to either the second or third of these senses of Rahner's rule.

For while, as we have seen, our salvation comes from God in the most undiminished sense, Calvin also jealously preserves the sovereignty of God, his freedom. To assert, as a statement of identity, that the immanent Trinity is the economic Trinity jeopardises that sovereignty, for it implies that there could be no other way or form of human salvation than the way that we know, that revealed in the one salvific intent of the three Trinitarian persons. As we saw earlier, Calvin is at pains to preserve the distinction between God as he is in himself and God as he is towards us. But how far may the distinction God *in se* and God *quoad nos* be pressed?

As we have seen, Calvin's stresses that God is a simple essence and (in his endorsement of Exodus 34.6) morally immaculate. So he could not subscribe to the idea that the relation between the economic Trinity and the immanent Trinity is an arbitrary or potentially mis-leading one. His reasoning, both with respect to the begottenness of the Son and to the procession of the Spirit, is that God necessarily reveals himself to us in a way that expresses his essential nature. So the activities of the first express the nature or character of the second. And we can see this, according to Calvin, because while the history of God's revelation culminates in the Incarnation, in the course of that revela-tion God unveils himself in non-incarnational ways. In this sense he is, despite the protestations of Karl Barth to the contrary, a 'God in general'.[41] However, there can be no inconsistency between God as he is and what is revealed about him in respect of human redemption.

So while in the interests of preserving divine freedom for Calvin we must not identify the immanent and economic Trinities, these 'Trinities' are closely allied, the one faithfully expressing the character of the other. But for Calvin, God could have acted differently, as we shall see when we discuss his view of the atonement, and so it is necessary to continue to distinguish between the immanent and the economic Trinities.

CALVIN: EASTERN OR WESTERN?

We have noted Calvin's emphasis on the equality of the Trinitarian per-sons, on the fact that each is *autotheos*. Some theologians have appealed to this as evidence that Calvin drew on Eastern, Cappadocian influ-ences for his account of the Trinity. And as we have seen there is one place in which Calvin does refer explicitly to Gregory of Nazianzen[42] as well as to Basil and to Athanasius.[43] T. F. Torrance says that

Calvin directs the reader for further explanation to the fifth book of Augustine's work on the *Trinity*, but actually he takes his chief cue from Gregory Nazianzen, with whom he sides in his evident disagreement with his friends Basil and Gregory Nyssen. Thus in spite of his judicious deployment of citations from Augustine, the recognised *magister theologiae* of the West, Calvin's trinitarian convictions were actually rather closer to those of the Greek Fathers Athanasius, Gregory Nazianzen, and Cyril of Alexandria.[44]

But as Anthony Lane has shown in detail, the idea of such influences must remain speculative since there is no hard evidence that Calvin read their writings,[45] whereas we do know that he consulted Augustine's *On the Trinity*, whose influence pervades other aspects of his theology. It is therefore reasonable to take the view that Calvin's ideas on the Trinity were strongly influenced by Augustine. In any case, despite the dust that is currently raised about the differences between 'western' and 'Cappadocian' views of the Trinity they are, after all, views of the same Christian doctrine, and so it is reasonable to expect the presence of important common features. The views of Calvin and the Cappadocians may reasonably be thought to coincide at certain points; there may even be some general unspecifiable Eastern influence, but Warfield is surely on safer ground when he states,

If distinctions must be drawn, he is unmistakably Western rather than Eastern in his conception of the doctrine, an Augustinian rather than an Athanasian. That is to say, the principle of his construction of the Trinitarian distinctions is equalization rather than subordination.[46]

If Calvin were to be asked on what he preferred, Origenesque subordinationism or Cappadocian *perichoresis*, then it is not hard to guess the answer. He would unhesitatingly have chosen *perichoresis*. But there are more alternatives than these two; while Calvin emphasises the coequality of the persons, an emphasis characteristic of Cappadocian *perichoresis*, he also favours an understanding of the Trinity that is not 'social', for (with Augustine) he emphasises the unity and indeed the simplicity of the godhead in whom the Trinity are three equally divine persons.

CHAPTER 4

THE SON

In this chapter we shall narrow our attention further in order to focus upon the centre of Calvin's understanding of the way to the true knowledge of God, as this is made possible, and actual, through the person and the work of Jesus Christ. It is not an accident that at the outset of his treatment of Christ's work Calvin once more links the knowledge we have of ourselves and the need for atonement.

> For seeing no man can descend into himself, and seriously consider what he is, without feeling that God is angry and at enmity with him, and therefore anxiously longing for the means of regaining his favour (this cannot be without satisfaction).[1]

Theologically speaking, the subject matter here begins to take us to the heart of things and to the centre of Calvin's creative genius. Although Calvin did not invent the threefold characterisation of Christ as Prophet, Priest and King, he is distinctive in the way he used it as a way of organising his theological thought.

> Therefore, that faith may find in Christ a solid ground of salvation, and so rest in him, we must set out with this principle, that the office which he received from the Father consists of three parts. For he was appointed both Prophet, King, and Priest; though little were gained by holding the names unaccompanied by a knowledge of the end and use. These, too, are spoken of in the Papacy, but frigidly, and with no great benefit, the full meaning comprehended under each title not being understood.[2]

When sketching Calvin's main Christological ideas, we shall try to follow this understanding of Christ's offices.

More innovative is Calvin's proposal that Christ is the author of a 'double grace', and that the Pauline theme of the believer's union with Christ by his Spirit is the means by which this grace is applied to those so united.

The whole may be thus summed up: Christ given to us by the kindness of God is apprehended and possessed by faith, by means of which we obtain in particular a twofold benefit: first, being reconciled by the righteousness of Christ, God becomes, instead of a judge, an indulgent Father; and, secondly, being sanctified by his Spirit, we aspire to integrity and purity of life.[3]

We cannot discuss all these issues at once, so in this chapter we shall attend first to the person of Christ, and to his priestly atonement, and then to his 'double grace'. Chapters 5 and 6 concern Christ's work as Prophet and King. Union with Christ, on which the 'double gift' hinges, is also fundamental to Calvin's understanding of the two sacraments, Baptism and the Lord's Supper, to which we shall come in Chapter 7.

THE CHALCEDONIAN BACKGROUND

Although as we have noted Calvin does not ascribe divine authority to Councils of the Church, but only to Scripture, nonetheless he pays due regard to them as affording the results of careful Christian deliberation, and therefore carrying a kind of subordinate authority. He discusses the authority of Councils at length in Book IV of the *Institutes* (Chapter 9). We noted his reservations over the Nicene Creed in Chapter 3. His Christology must be understood not only in terms of the Scriptural witness but also as employing the conceptuality of the Council of Chalcedon in AD 451.

According to the Chalcedonian view, the Incarnation is a union of two natures, divine and human, and each retains its essential character in the union. This may seem an obvious point but it, or its implications, has often been contested.

[We also teach] that we apprehend this one and only Christ – Son, Lord, only-begotten – in two natures; [and we do this] without

54

confusing the two natures, without transmuting one nature into the other, without dividing them into two separate categories, without contrasting them according to area or function. The distinctiveness of each nature is not nullified by the union.[4]

That is, whatever properties that are essential to God being God – for example, omnipotence or omniscience – in becoming Incarnate in the Son, God cannot abdicate these properties. Perhaps the God-man could refrain from *manifesting* his omnipotence through his human nature, but he certainly cannot give up or empty himself of it. For in giving it up he would cease to be God, and there would as a consequence be no true Incarnation. As Calvin puts it, 'For, in order to exhort us to submission by his example, he shows, that when as God he might have displayed to the world the brightness of his glory, he gave up his right, and voluntarily emptied himself; that he assumed the form of a servant, and, contented with that humble condition, suffered his divinity to be concealed under a veil of flesh.'[5]

THE MEDIATOR

Calvin did not regard Chalcedonian Christology as an *explanation* of the mystery of the Incarnation but as encompassing what, in the light of the Scriptural revelation, is essential to it and what is denied by it. Calvin endorsed the central thrust of Chalcedon, as this comment on John 1.14 show:

On this article of faith there are two things chiefly to be observed. The first is, that two natures were so united in one Person in Christ, that one and the same Christ is true God and true man. The second is, that the unity of person does not hinder the two natures from remaining distinct, so that his Divinity retains all that is peculiar to itself, and his humanity holds separately whatever belongs to it. . . . On the other hand, since he distinctly gives to the man Christ the name of *the Speech*, it follows that Christ, when he became man, did not cease to be what he formerly was, and that no change took place in that eternal essence of God which was clothed with *flesh*.[6]

Here are some of the expressions that Calvin uses to convey the union of the divine person and human nature in the Incarnation while at the same time preserving the distinctness of each: the Son of God 'assumed' human nature, he was 'clothed with flesh', divinity and human nature were mutually connected; 'he took our nature upon himself'; he 'came forth as true man and took the person and the name of Adam'; he 'coupled human nature with divine'.[7] But since the Son of God is essentially God and is thus (for example) impassible, immense and omnipresent, he must remain in his Incarnation impassible, immense and omnipresent. Consequently, whatever account may be given of the person of Jesus Christ, and of the connectedness of humanity and divinity in that one person, the relation of the divine to the human is asymmetrical – in the Incarnation, the eternal God takes on human nature but human nature does not take on the divine.

Therefore, as the Incarnation cannot involve an intrinsic change in the divine nature, it follows that it must involve a new relationship between the Logos and human nature, as when a man in becoming a father has a new relationship but does not cease to be a man. But if the Incarnation is such a relationship, in what sense can Christ be wholly divine? The answer to this must have due regard to divine simplicity. Because God is simple the Son of God is simple, without parts, necessarily wholly divine, and he cannot be partly in union with human nature, and partly not, since he has no parts. In the union, Christ's deity is undiminished. He has parts in an extended sense, the sense in which (for Calvin at least) a human being is part body, part soul. Calvin is very fond of the analogy between the human body and soul and Christ's becoming incarnate in human nature.[8] So although human nature is part of the God-man, human nature is not a part of the Logos.

Yet, although his human nature is not a part of the Logos (since the Logos, being God, has no parts), it is also a consequence of the simplicity and immensity of the Logos that he is not confined within the bounds of human nature in the way in which (according to Calvin) a particular human soul is situated within a particular human body. Just as according to Calvin the Logos is simple and immense, so the human nature of Christ is necessarily spatially circumscribed. It is for this reason that Calvin endorses Peter Lombard's 'trite' distinction that although the whole Christ is everywhere, still the whole of that which is in him is not everywhere.[9] This states, conversely, that the Son of God is omnipresent, but Christ's human nature, which is 'in' him by virtue of his union with the Son (although not, of course, physically or spatially in him) cannot be omnipresent.

Calvin also seems to imply that we must not infer from the fact that God is omnipresent that wherever God is present he is equally present, but that there may be different intensities of God's presence. Or perhaps his view is that God's presence may be experienced in different ways according to the receptive powers of the recipient. Calvin is careful not to say that because God is omnipresent and he is equally present to the human nature of Jesus and to the human nature of anyone else. He says that

> In this way, both the Son of man was in heaven because he was also Christ; and he who, according to the flesh, dwelt as the Son of man on earth, was also God in heaven. For this reason, he is said to have descended from heaven in respect of his divinity, not that his divinity quitted heaven to conceal itself in the prison of the body, but because, although he filled all things, it yet resided in the humanity of Christ corporeally, that is, naturally, and in an ineffable manner.[10]

So in virtue of his divinity the Son of God is omnipresent and thus present to the whole of his creation. But he is 'present' to his human nature in a very different sense, in the sense that it is *his* human nature in a way in which you and I are not his human nature; that, for example, he can move his own hands and feet in a manner that he cannot move someone else's hands and feet, and has his own stream of consciousness in a way that he does not 'possess' mine or yours.

Of course, in drawing attention to the ineffability of this union Calvin is not going beyond what Christian theologians, including the scholastics, have always said about the mystery of the Incarnation. Calvin's precise point is that the truth of the Incarnation is beyond reason in the sense that it is not explicable in the way that other kinds of union or unity may be, because it is *sui generis*, a union of the divine and the human.

Calvin characteristically handles the problems posed by the union of Christ's divine person and human nature by claiming that it is the one Mediator, Jesus Christ, to whom both divine and human predicates are to be ascribed. For example, it is the Mediator who has two wills; it is not that one will possesses another will. It is the Mediator who (in his divine nature) knows all things but who (in his human nature) is ignorant of certain matters. In effect Calvin endorses a set of 'grammatical' rules about what can and cannot be said about both the distinctness of the natures and the unity of the God-man, endeavouring in these rules to follow the Scriptural witness and that alone.[11]

One reason for holding together, as one, the union of the natures in the person and work of the Mediator, is that Calvin held that the work of Mediator can only be performed by the one God-man. In the case of Christ's Mediatorship both the Son of God and that human nature to which he is united exemplify instances of the same moral and spiritual predicates; the Son of God essentially and infinitely so, in virtue of his divinity, the human nature contingently and finitely so, in view of its creation in God's image. By virtue of the union of the two natures the moral and spiritual properties of God himself are communicated in measure to the human nature of Christ.

So in his Christology, Calvin focusses on the divine economy; it is in virtue of his role as Mediator of salvation that the Son of God, uniting with human nature, communicated to that nature (by the Spirit?) those graces by which Christ could effect salvation. 'Neither could they be attributed to one who was a man and nothing more.'[12]

Calvin's commitment to the Chalcedonian emphasis on the unchanging character of the two natures of Christ aroused controversy at the time of the Reformation, particularly in connection with rival understandings of the Lord's Supper. Calvin and the Calvinian party resisted the Lutheran view that in the Incarnation Christ's human nature itself took on divine properties, such as immensity, through what is referred to as the *communicatio idiomatum*, the communication of properties. Calvin denied this understanding of the *communicatio* and could give conciliar and Patristic precedent for his denial.

But he did not reject the very idea of the communication of properties, because Scripture contains passages where human properties are ascribed to God and (he believed) divine properties are ascribed to man. 'Let us, therefore, regard it as the key of true interpretation, that those things which refer to the office of Mediator are not spoken of the divine or human nature simply.'[13]

So the *communicatio* is a hermeneutical or grammatical rule that enables us to understand certain unusual texts of Scripture in a way that displays their coherence with the rest. It is possible to speak of

Mary as the mother of the Lord (Luke 1.43) and of Christ's blood as the blood of God (Acts 20.28) and of the Lord of glory as being crucified (1 Cor. 2.8). How can this be, when God does not have a mother, nor blood, nor can the Lord of glory be crucified? Calvin's answer is that these are vivid and economical ways of speaking warranted by the unity of the divine and human natures of the Mediator and nothing more.

However, we break this hermeneutical rule, extending it beyond its proper bounds, if we say that God literally shed his blood or that Mary was literally the mother of God. Calvin insists that these – having blood, having a mother – are properties of the one Mediator. The language of the *communicatio* is thus based upon or warranted by the nature of the Incarnation, even when there is no explicit, exclusive reference to the Mediator.

It follows that the language of *communicatio*, though sanctioned by Scripture, is nevertheless figurative, metaphorical or 'improper', whenever it occurs.

CALVIN AND THE ATONEMENT

We now turn our attention to Christ's work and first to his priesthood.

In his great work *Cur Deus Homo* Anselm of Canterbury (1033–1109) argued that given God's intention to restore humanity, atonement by God was necessary in virtue of the depth of human sin, and that atonement must be made by the God-man in order to restore human nature. Whether or not Calvin was directly influenced by Anselm – and it seems likely that he was not – he nevertheless uses Anselmian language to characterise the atonement. He rarely quotes or refers to Anselm directly. In fact there is only one quotation from him in the *Institutes*, but this has no connection with the atonement.[14] Since in drawing attention to Calvin's Anselmianism no direct literary influence is evident, perhaps the true explanation of Calvin's language is simply that Anselmianism was 'in the air' in the circles in which he first learned theology, and that he came to believe that this outlook fairly expressed the biblical view.

But Calvin is not straightforwardly Anselmian because, rather surprisingly, we find two views of the atonement, and two views of the necessity of the atonement, side by side in Calvin's writings. The first, the main view, is to be found expounded *in extenso* in the *Institutes* and elsewhere and is expressed by the following representative statements.

It deeply concerned us, that he who was to be our Mediator should be very God and very man. If the necessity be inquired into, it was not what is commonly called simple or absolute, but flowed from the divine decree on which the salvation of man depended. What was best for us, our most merciful Father determined. . . . The case was certainly desperate, if the Godhead itself did not descend to us, it being impossible for us to ascend. Thus the Son of God behoved to become our Emmanuel, *i.e.* God with us.[15]

He writes of the necessity of the atonement, that it is 'required', and that the atonement must be undertaken by the very majesty of God himself in the person of the Son becoming Immanuel. 'Even had Adam not lost his integrity, he would, with the angels, have been like to God; and yet it would not therefore have been necessary that the Son of God should become either a man or an angel.'[16] This was in reply to the Lutheran, Andreas Osiander (1498–1565), who to Calvin's extreme annoyance held that if Adam had not sinned the Incarnation would nevertheless have occurred. Note that Osiander's claim is not that there could be atonement without incarnation (and so without blood shedding) but that there could have been incarnation without atonement. Calvin denied this, claiming that the Incarnation was a gracious response to human sin.

But does Calvin go to the other extreme, voluntarism? Does the fact that the necessity of the Incarnation, for Calvin, 'stemmed from a heavenly decree' undermine the Anselmianism? Is the heavenly decree to be understood as governing the fact of reconciliation or the nature of the reconciliation? If the first, then Calvin's Anselmianism is at once compromised. In the passage just cited, at least, Calvin appears to conflate the two. However, this stress on the heavenly decree is taken up later in a passage which several commentators have understood in a non-Anselmian way.

For Christ could not merit anything save by the good pleasure of God, but only inasmuch as he was destined to appease the wrath of God by his sacrifice, and wipe away our transgressions by his obedience: in one word, since the merit of Christ depends entirely on the grace of God (which provided this mode of salvation for us), the latter is no less appropriately opposed to all righteousness of men than is the former.[17]

But the point made here is in fact identical to that just discussed, and not, I believe, susceptible of a non-Anselmian interpretation as regards the mode of atonement. The words don't imply that the meritoriousness of Christ's atonement is due solely to God's decision that it be meritorious. Rather, Calvin is saying that we benefit from Christ's merit because it was God's will that we should. Nevertheless, in the reference to the heavenly decree of *Institutes* II.12.1, perhaps Calvin is hinting at the decidedly unAnselmian idea that God could have decreed redemption in another way, a view we shall shortly hear more of. Even if this is so, we need not think that Calvin holds that God's acceptance of some action as meritorious is sufficient for it to be meritorious, the doctrine of *acceptio* that originates with the mediaeval theologian Duns Scotus. What is 'best for us' is what is the best way of delivering us from our plight, and the point of what follows in the *Institutes* is to establish that only the descent of the very majesty of God would manage that.

In these extracts Calvin conflates two questions, seeing no need to separate them. First, in order for there to be pardon for sin, and so reconciliation between God and man, did there have to be an atonement? To this Calvin gives an affirmative answer. Second, given that there had to be an atonement, who could provide the atonement of the sort that is necessary? Calvin answers: only the God-man, who was destined for this role by the grace of God. These questions are strictly speaking distinct, for it is possible to suppose that an answer to the question 'If there is to be salvation must there be an atonement?' should be answered affirmatively, but that there be a number of alternative possible answers to the question 'Who then may atone?' But Calvin takes the question as one question, not as two. One might press the issue further by asking what must constitute the act of atonement? But as far as I am aware Calvin does not raise this further question.

In order to help clarify matters in the discussions that are to follow, let us make some distinctions. Terms such as 'hypothetical' and 'necessary' in regard to the atonement have been variously used. In order to clarify the subsequent discussion the following distinctions are necessary.

(1) Necessarily, given creation and Fall, there is to be reconciliation via the God-man.

(2) Necessarily, if there is to be reconciliation, then it will be by atonement by the God-man.

(3) If there is to be reconciliation, then possibly it will be by atonement by the God-man.

I shall call (1) the *absolute* view, (2) the *necessary* view and (3) the *hypothetical* view of the atonement. Only (2) and (3) are relevant to our discussion, since no party in this debate, certainly no view attributable to Calvin, subscribes to (1), since reconciliation is regarded by him as a free action of God. It is not an absolutely necessary matter that there be salvation at all, and given that reconciliation arises from God's decree or decision there are necessary and hypothetical variants of this – reconciliation that necessitates atonement/satisfaction or in some other way.

In my view, in the *Institutes* Calvin uniformly (though by implication) denies (3) and explicitly affirms (2), as this passage (among many others) indicates.

> Another principal part of our reconciliation with God was, that man, who had lost himself by his disobedience, should by way of remedy, oppose to it obedience, satisfy the justice of God, and pay the penalty of sin. Therefore, our Lord came forth very man, adopted the person of Adam, and assumed his name, that he might in his stead obey the Father; that he might present our flesh as the price of satisfaction to the just judgment of God, and in the same flesh pay the penalty which we had incurred. Finally, since as God only he could not suffer, and as man only could not overcome death, he united the human nature with the divine, that he might subject the weakness of the one to death as an expiation of sin, and by the power of the other, maintaining a struggle with death, might gain us the victory.[18]

This statement of Calvin's regarding the necessity of the atonement and the necessity of the eternal Son atoning by taking on human nature has a decidedly Anselmian ring. Each corresponds in turn to the main two features of Anselm's project in *Cur Deus Homo,* that atonement is necessary for pardon and that only atonement by the God-man is sufficient.

So far we may say that Calvin's approach to the atonement is Anselmian in its basic logic. However, there are several important respects in which Calvin is *not* Anselmian. First, and most obviously, he does not argue *remoto Christo*, as if Christ had never been. Quite the contrary. In committing himself to the necessity of the atonement Calvin is, or believes that he is, simply summarising the Scriptural record regarding Christ and his work. Anselm's project was to argue a priori for the necessity of the atonement claiming that any atonement considered as a reconciliation of God and mankind had to have a certain character. By contrast, Calvin proceeds a posteriori, from the revealed data. This is not a mere accidental difference. Calvin would not have been in sympathy with an a priori approach to the question, because of its potential for speculation, and because of the way in which such an approach takes its leave of the text of Scripture. He explicitly makes the point about the need to avoid speculation in his polemic against Osiander.

He who considers these things with due attention, will easily disregard vague speculations, which attract giddy minds and lovers of novelty. One speculation of this class is, that Christ, even though there had been no need of his interposition to redeem the human race, would still have become man.[19]

Connected with this a priori emphasis in Anselm is his characteristic appeal to 'reason', his attempt to uncover the underlying rationale of a revealed doctrine. Calvin is much more cautious, attempting to adhere to the biblical data and what they imply. So we might say that Calvin takes up some of Anselm's conclusions, in particular that the atonement is necessary in our sense (2), without endorsing his arguments for those conclusions.

Apart from this, on the evidence of *Institutes* II.12.5 Calvin is simply making the point that to consider whether incarnation apart from atonement is possible is speculative in the face of statements of Scripture showing that they are 'joined together by God's eternal decree' to redeem the elect. Further, it is I believe unwarranted to assume that the reference to a Mediator in Calvin's statement 'Had man remained free from all taint, he was of too humble a condition to penetrate to God without a Mediator'[20] is a reference to the Incarnation. As we have noted, for Calvin 'divine Mediatorship' is a generic term of which Mediatorship by Incarnation is one species. On the other hand, no proposal that there might be atonement in some other way without divine satisfaction is in view here or elsewhere in the *Institutes*.

Finally, in establishing the necessity of the atonement Calvin does not proceed from the nature of God viewed abstractly (as Anselm did) but rather from the character of the Incarnation itself. He denies that there has been an absolute necessity (our sense (1)) for the Mediator to be both true God and true man, but one that flowed from the divine decree. That is, it does not follow as a matter of logic from the fact of the Fall and of universal human sinfulness that there must be an atonement for that sin. Rather it follows solely from the divine decree, a decree that is free but which, for Calvin, must reflect and expresses God's character. Hence 'mere gratuitous love prompts him to receive us into favour'.[21]

So he avoids the more basic question of whether the atonement was necessary simply in view of the fact that mankind had sinned. That would be to give the atonement an 'absolute' necessity, our sense (1). Nevertheless he could in theory have argued that though the atonement was not absolutely necessary (in sense (1)) yet granted that it is the free, non-necessitated divine intention to provide one, that atonement could have been other than via the Incarnation of the Son of God. But he does not think in this fashion, and (as we have seen) he conflates the two questions: Must there be an atonement? And, must Christ atone? into an affirmative answer to the second. This is usually taken to be Anselm's view as regards the Incarnation.

A SECOND CALVIN?

However, there is another side to Calvin's idea of the atonement, expressions of which may be found in his sermons and commentaries, represented in the following statements:

> For if God had simply proclaimed our pardon by declaring that he had decided to receive us in mercy, despite our unworthiness, that would have been a great thing. Even then, we would never have been able to utter sufficient praise for such grace. But God has given us his own Son as a token of his love. Indeed, he has given us himself through his Son, and declared himself to be our Father. This so far outshines pardon alone that even if we employed all our faculties to worship and adore, we could never perfectly praise him for such mercy.[22]

If God pardoned us without Jesus Christ interceding for us and being made our pledge, we should think nothing of it. We should all shrug our shoulders and make it an opportunity for giving ourselves greater license. But when we see that God did not spare His only Son, but treated Him with such an extreme severity that in His Body He underwent all the sorrows that it would be possible to suffer and then even in His soul He was afflicted to the limit, to the point of crying out 'My God, my God, why hast thou forsaken me?' – when we hear all this, it is impossible for us, unless we are harder than stone, not to shudder and be filled with such a fear and amazement as will utterly put us to confusion; impossible not to detest our offences and iniquities seeing that they provoke the anger of God against us in this way. This, then, is why it was necessary for all the correction of our peace to be laid upon Jesus Christ that we might find grace before God His Father.[23]

How are we to understand these decidedly unAnselmian sentences? I think we can rule out the idea that Calvin changed his mind on the question. For one thing, the Anselmianism of the *Institutes* is affirmed in the last (1559) edition. But perhaps the *Institutes* testifies to some hardening of Calvin's position in the direction of Anselmianism, prompted by his correspondence with Laelius Socinus, as I argued in *John Calvin's Ideas*. Yet the writings from which we have just quoted cannot be easily assigned to an 'earlier' or 'later' Calvin. The *Sermons on Galatians* were delivered in 1557 and published in 1563, those on Isaiah 53 have a similar date, 1556, after his exchanges with the older Socinus which came to an end in 1555. Throughout these years Calvin was preparing the definitive edition of the *Institutes*. Nowhere does he repudiate a view of the atonement that he once held, neither in these passages nor elsewhere does he express a sense of dissonance between them and the view expressed in the *Institutes*.

How are we to understand this puzzling state of affairs: two apparently dissonant approaches to the atonement, but one that Calvin did not (apparently) notice? Is he guilty of a logical *faux pas* about a fundamental aspect of his teaching without seeing it? I shall try to argue that it is possible to harmonise these two points of view.

The views of the 'second Calvin' have their source in Augustine, and are also to be found in Thomas Aquinas, and no doubt in others. Not that these two affirmed the possibility of salvation by 'a word', but they deny the necessity of the atonement, or, in the case of

Thomas, he denies the necessity of a necessary condition of the Anselmian view of the atonement, the Incarnation.

Thomas discusses the Incarnation in *Summa Theologiae* 3a 1–6, and among the questions he considers is, Was the Incarnation necessary for the restoration of the human race? Citing Augustine in support he says,

> We refer to something as necessary for an end in two senses. First, when the goal is simply unattainable without it, e.g. food for sustaining human life. Second, when it is required for a better and more expeditious attainment of the goal, e.g. a horse for a journey. In the first sense the Incarnation was not necessary for the restoration of human nature, since by his infinite power God had many other ways to accomplish this end. In the second sense, however, it was needed for the restoration of human nature.

> Accordingly, Augustine writes, *Let us point out that other ways were not wanting to God, whose power rules everything without exception, yet that there was no other course more fitting for healing our wretchedness.*[24]

It may be that what Aquinas claims gives us a way of harmonising Calvin. What he says implies that any view of atonement that requires the Incarnation (as Anselm's view of the atonement does) is not necessary. Is this compatible with salvation 'by a word'? Perhaps it is. Such a way of salvation may be among the 'many other ways' that God had of accomplishing the restoration of human nature.

Here is my suggestion. Overall, Calvin is interested not only in the end of atonement – pardon, reconciliation – as if this could be understood abstractly, but also and perhaps chiefly in the connection of means and ends. For him there are not two equivalently alternative means to one end, pardon and reconciliation, which God might indifferently choose between. That would be clearly voluntaristic. Rather, Calvin thinks that there are alternative ends with alternative means; in each case there is a conceptual or internal connection between means and ends.

There are possible schemes of atonement in which the love of God is not maximally expressed. For Calvin there is only one possible way of God maximally expressing his love, namely atonement by the Incarnation of the Logos and satisfaction by the death of the

God-man. For the Incarnation and satisfaction of divine justice by the God-man, and much else, are in his view logically necessary and jointly sufficient for procuring those precise, rich benefits which (Calvin understood the New Testament to teach) we in fact enjoy. There may have been another way to pay the price of sin, or rather *not* to pay the price of sin but to freely pardon it. But there was no other way of procuring those God-glorifying effects that fill us with wonder and amazement at the character of God's love.

If it is God's will that we are to enjoy such specific, maximal blessings, then we cannot enjoy them without they come to us in a manner which ensures them, and which gives them their distinctive character, and to achieve this requires Incarnation and atonement of a broadly Anselmian kind. Yet quite unlike Anselm, Calvin starts not with a relatively abstract view of reconciliation, but with the concrete blessings of being in Christ, and then asks: what does being in union with Christ in this sense require on the part of God? His answer is clear: it requires Incarnation, propitiatory death of the incarnate Son rendering satisfaction to divine justice, resurrection, ascension and session, along with the applicatory work of the Spirit bringing men and women to the position of being 'in Christ'. Only by presupposing all this can the distinctive Pauline blessings of union with Christ, which (as we shall shortly see) Calvin so notably emphasises, be ensured.

If this is the true account of Calvin's views, then we must say this: Calvin briefly, but several times, expresses the opinion that an alternative outcome could have been decreed with good reason by God. But he quickly moves on, impelled by what he understands to be the Scriptural account of what actually happened. Though pardon by fiat is abstractly possible, the reconciliation that would ensue would have been a thin thing. If the reconciliation is to be that which befits the majesty, goodness and grace of God and maximally benefits us, then it must be undertaken and procured by the God-man.

For Calvin what is 'best for us' is not merely that we are pardoned and received back into the favour of God, but that we are pardoned through the person and work of the God-man. Pressing the Anselmian parallel a little further, we might say that Calvin thinks that that view of reconciliation and salvation is most fitting which maximally benefits us and maximally honours God our Redeemer, as expressed in this double superlative: 'What was best for us, our most merciful Father determined.'[25] Such an atonement is one than which no better can be conceived.

CHRIST'S ATONEMENT

We must now consider the nature of Christ's atonement that Calvin favours and begin by considering his attitude to Christ's merit.

We have noted just now the voluntarism (or perhaps non-necessitarianism) of certain of Calvin's statements about the status of the atonement. Some commentators have also seen elements of voluntarism in what Calvin has to say about the nature of the atonement in the *Institutes*. They think that here as elsewhere aspects of Duns Scotus's idea of *acceptio*, the view that whether or not an action has merit is not a feature of the sort of action it is but depends solely on the divine 'acceptance' of that action thus giving it value, are discernible. So on such a view Christ's sacrifice is meritorious, or perhaps meritorious *for us,* only because God decreed it to be so. Not otherwise.

The noted Calvin commentator François Wendel quotes from a section of the *Institutes* where Calvin says, 'Therefore, when we treat of the merit of Christ, we do not place the beginning in him, but we ascend to the ordination of God as the primary cause, because of his mere good pleasure he appointed a Mediator to purchase salvation for us.'[26] Wendel claims that this amounts to saying that Christ was able to deserve our salvation only because God would have it so.[27] This is not in any case quite equivalent to the view that God could have pardoned by declaring us pardoned. For it may still be possible to hold that Christ's atonement was necessary, but not sufficient, to effect atonement. What is also necessary, on this view, is the divine *acceptio*. Maybe atonement by Christ was fitting, perhaps the only fitting way to address human sin, yet not intrinsically meritorious. This is perhaps what Wendel means. Or perhaps it is that God accepts an atonement that is less than what strict justice requires. This is also possible, but there is little or no evidence that this is Calvin's view.

But there is another, more obvious way to understand what Calvin says. In the context from which Wendel quotes he is discussing and rejecting the views of those who would 'insist that Christ was only the instrument or minister, not the author or leader, or prince of life, as he is designated by Peter (Acts 3.15)'. Calvin rejects the view that Christ is a mere executive of the divine will and not himself one who wills our salvation from the beginning. What is his argument? He cites Augustine to the effect that the man Christ Jesus is predestined by God to be the Saviour. The merit of Christ's human nature did not originate with him; it was not as if the Son had to wrest salvation from an unwilling Father.

It is absurd to set Christ's merit against God's mercy. Christ's human nature was not united to the divine person because it deserved to be, but solely because of God's predestining grace. Calvin is not saying that Christ had merit simply by divine fiat – the fiat of God is not under discussion – but that he has the office of Mediator because he was predestined to it by God's love for us. There is therefore no opposition between the grace of God and the office of Christ, for Christ has his office because God destined him to it. Christ is God's free gift, and the merit of Christ is intrinsic to that gift.

So at the heart of Calvin's view of the atonement is the idea of Christ's merit procured by his obedience even to the death of the cross. By that obedience he satisfied divine justice. Here is Calvin developing the Anselmic logic of the atonement in style.

> Therefore, our Lord came forth very man, adopted the person of Adam, and assumed his name, that he might in his stead obey the Father; that he might present our flesh as the price of satisfaction to the just judgment of God, and in the same flesh pay the penalty which we had incurred. Finally, since as God only he could not suffer, and as man only could not overcome death, he united the human nature with the divine, that he might subject the weakness of the one to death as an expiation of sin, and by the power of the other, maintaining a struggle with death, might gain us the victory.[28]

We see here how closely he connects Christ's satisfaction for sin and the substitution of himself in our place.

> It had been superfluous and therefore absurd, that Christ should have been burdened with a curse, had it not been in order that, by paying what others owed, he might acquire righteousness for them . . . For had not Christ satisfied for our sins, he could not be said to have appeased God by taking upon himself the penalty which we had incurred.[29]

Summing this up, we may say that Calvin favours a penal substitutionary view of the atonement.[30] Sometimes, it is true, he seems to settle for a satisfaction view, at other times he conflates the two without caring or noticing.[31] But whether the correct label is 'satisfaction' or 'substitution' we don't fully capture his thought with either. Christ is the conquering king, our victor. Equally fundamental, perhaps, is the dramatic character of the atonement. By offering Christ as our Saviour in this way the Lord wishes to display, in a vivid, heart-breaking and yet heart-warming way, how much he loves us.

It is fair to say that later Reformed theologians were rattled by the rise of Socinianism, with its taunting question, 'Why could not God have saved us by a word of clemency, as we forgive those that injure us?' Their response was to stress the centrality of divine vindicatory justice. Because of the need to vindicate divine justice, the cross had to be the way. That is straight Anselmianism. Of course we can only guess, but Calvin might well have said that in giving this answer the Reformed theologians had missed an opportunity. The focus should not be on what God had to do, but on what he wanted to do. He could have saved us by a word. He wanted to show how much he loved us, to break our hearts. And what was the best way of doing this? By himself coming in human nature for our redemption and uniting us to him in death and resurrection.

CHRIST'S TWOFOLD GIFT

One consequence of Calvin upholding the full divinity of the incarnate Word is that Christ's death, because it is the death of the God-man, merits our salvation; by contrast, we ourselves because of our mere creatureliness and our sin are incapable of meriting anything. But what did Christ in fact merit for us? What are these maximally beneficial gifts that God the Father provides for us through the work of God the Son? The answer to these questions takes us to the heart of Calvin's understanding of how Christ benefits us. He puts it this way.

These blessings are conjoined by a perpetual and inseparable tie. Those whom he enlightens by his wisdom he redeems; whom he redeems he justifies; whom he justifies he sanctifies. But as the question relates only to justification and sanctification, to them let us confine ourselves. Though we distinguish between them, they are both inseparably comprehended in Christ. Would ye then obtain justification in Christ? You must previously possess Christ. But you cannot possess him without being made a partaker of his sanctification; for Christ cannot be divided.[32]

So from Christ we receive a double gift. Calvin's basic thought, as he moves from considering the work of Christ to how that work is applied to us and affects us, is that by the unspeakable mercy of God we are united to Christ, and from that one 'mystical' union two distinct but inseparable benefits flow. He has a favourite illustration to help us. He says that Christ is like the sun from which we receive both light and heat. Light is not heat and heat is not light, but each comes from the same source and each is inseparable from the other. Likewise justification (the reckoning of a person's righteous in God's sight) is not sanctification (the renewing of a person's character by Christ's indwelling Spirit) and sanctification is not justification, but each of these comes from the one Christ as by God's grace we are united to him.

It is important to grasp that for Calvin this union with Christ does not depend on anything we do or have, not even on our faith. It is God's immediate, gracious donation. Christ is given to us to be grasped by faith; faith (another gift of God) is our response, it is not what procures the gift in the first place. From the gift springs 'the special life which Christ breathes into his people, that they may be one with him'.[33]

This stress on Christ's one two-aspect gift is, I believe, a stroke of genius. The religious consequences of this conceptuality cannot be exaggerated. In what is essentially a refinement of Luther's view of justification by faith alone through the 'alien' righteousness of Christ, Calvin's doctrine of the double grace breaks apart the mediaeval idea that justification is moral renewal. No, says Calvin, following Paul, justification is the declaring of a person to be righteous, and this is enjoyed by faith alone, as the righteousnss of Christ is imputed to the believer. But there is moral renewal, and it is inseparable from justification. For inseparably accompanying justification, as the second aspect of Christ's 'donation', is sanctification. Both justification and sanctification are the gifts of grace. They are not to be separated, but they are not to be confused, as the mediaeval church confused them with (Calvin believes) ultimately disastrous consequences.

In regard to vulgar Papists or Schoolmen, they are here doubly wrong, both in calling faith assurance of conscience while waiting to receive from God the reward of merits, and in interpreting

divine grace to mean not the imputation of gratuitous righteousness, but the assistance of the Spirit in the study of holiness.[34]

And even his hero Augustine erred about justification, if not about
merit.

Even the sentiment of Augustine, or at least his mode of expressing
it, cannot be entirely approved of. For although he is admirable in
stripping man of all merit of righteousness, and transferring the
whole praise of it to God, yet he classes the grace by which we are
regenerated to newness of life under the head of sanctification.[35]

Surprisingly Calvin does not make a song and a dance over what,
when it occurred in others, was a serious error. Why is this? Because
Calvin clearly believed that Augustine thought that 'justification'
(in Augustine's sense) – both justification and sanctification in Calvin's
sense – are entirely the result of divine grace alone. So a failure clearly
to understand Paul's forensic, declarative sense of 'justify', through
a mistranslation of the original, though a mistake, is not of itself fatal.
But it becomes fatal if the Augustinian meaning of 'justify' comes to
harbour false views of human merit, and so comes to be equivalent
to a version of salvation by human effort. It is then to be strenuously
resisted, because it undermines the biblical teaching of salvation by
grace alone. Augustine himself is clear that both faith and 'meritorious' works are gifts of God's grace – that is why Calvin is so muted in
his criticism of him – but in the late mediaeval church 'meritorious
works' had come to have a semi-Pelagian connotation or worse.

It is sometimes claimed that the differences between these two ideas
of justification are merely semantic. It is said that in the infusion
sense of acceptance or justification, justification (in the forensic sense)
and sanctification are simply rolled together, whereas on the other
view they are kept separate. Once we understand that point, it is said,
we shall see that the Reformation conflict was nothing more than an
argument about a word. But this is certainly not Calvin's view.

Why, then, are we justified by faith? Because by faith we apprehend
the righteousness of Christ, which alone reconciles us to God. This
faith, however, you cannot apprehend without at the same time
apprehending sanctification; for Christ 'is made unto us wisdom,

and righteousness, and sanctification, and redemption' (I Cor. 1.30). Christ, therefore, justifies no man without also sanctifying him. These blessings are conjoined by a perpetual and inseparable tie. Those whom he enlightens by his wisdom he redeems; whom he redeems he justifies; whom he justifies he sanctifies.[36]

So justification is down to faith alone. Not that faith is a ground or basis of justification; it is merely its instrument. 'We compare faith to a kind of vessel, because we are incapable of receiving Christ, unless we are emptied and come with open mouth to receive his grace'.[37] The basis of justification is the merit of Christ through whom we receive pardon and whose righteousness is imputed to us.

He, on the other hand, is justified who is regarded not as a sinner, but as righteous, and as such stands acquitted at the judgment-seat of God, where all sinners are condemned. As an innocent man, when charged before an impartial judge, who decides according to his innocence, is said to be justified by the judge, so a man is said to be justified by God when, removed from the catalogue of sinners, he has God as the witness and assertor of his righteousness. . . . On the contrary, a man will be *justified by faith* when, excluded from the righteousness of works, he by faith lays hold of the righteousness of Christ, and clothed in it appears in the sight of God not as a sinner, but as righteous . . . we say that this justification consists in the forgiveness of sins and the imputation of the righteousness of Christ.[38]

The crucial point, then, has to do with the grounding of justification. For Calvin, it is grounded in the alien righteousness of Christ imputed to us; for Augustine, its grounding includes the graciously given subjective renewal of the believer.

It is sometimes said that the very idea of the imputation of righteousness from one person to another is fictional. There would be some basis to the charge if Calvin held that it is Christ's subjective righteousness which is reckoned as our subjective righteousness. How would such an exchange be possible? But this is not what he means; rather, it is the merit of Christ that is reckoned to us, changing our moral and quasi-legal status before God from that of condemnation to that of vindication. When an orphan is adopted, or a fine paid for a penniless offender who is then discharged, this does not entail a change in character. The orphan is simply legally the true child of its new mother and father; the debt of the penniless offender is cancelled.

Nevertheless – and this is the beauty of Calvin's conception of the twofold gift – the justification that is appropriated by faith alone is inseparable from the reception of the second gift, sanctification, subjective moral and spiritual renewal. Such an orphan, adopted into the heavenly family, does not only become the child of his new Heavenly Father, but it is guaranteed that the child will become like the Father. The change of status and the change of subjective condition are bonded together, and are therefore not to be thought of as contingently connected, as the critics of the Reformation view of justification by faith alone claimed, who held that it encourages antinomianism.

We have been looking chiefly (though briefly) at justification, the first of the two inseparable graces with which Christ blesses and benefits men and women. More broadly, in this chapter we have been considering Christ's work as our Priest.[39] We shall look at the second aspect of Christ's gift, sanctification, in Chapters 5 and 6, which will require us to look at Christ's work as Prophet and King.

CHAPTER 5

GRACE AND FAITH

As our Prophet Christ rules us by his Word, and the chief way in which he does this, for Calvin, is that he teaches us so as to produce the true knowledge of God and of ourselves. We have seen that for Calvin sound doctrine – the sort that we have been reflecting on in the earlier chapters – benefits or profits us; it promotes true religion. The way in which it does this is by men and women, through the regenerating work of the Spirit, coming to rely upon God's word of promise. This promise concerns not only the remission of sins and the reckoning of Christ's righteousness to the believer but also individual moral and spiritual renewal and the conduct of the believer in society. The Calvinian treatment of the connection between sound doctrine and true religion will occupy us in Chapters 6 and 7.

JUSTIFICATION AND SANCTIFICATION

As we have already noted, for Calvin the attainment of salvation consists of two elements. The first is a changed status in which the believer is pardoned and receives Christ's righteousness imputed to him. This is *justification*, the provision of 'alien righteousness' that was a central feature of the Reformation cry of justification by faith only. The second element is subjective renewal, the renovation of a person's character through the instrumentality of Christ's Spirit and Christ's Word – *sanctification*. During Calvin's life, beginning with his debate with the Lutheran Andreas Osiander, for example, and following the pronouncements of the Council of Trent, the relationship between justification and sanctification became a matter of ongoing controversy and (I think it is fair to say) of some misunderstanding. Had both his followers and his opponents paid more attention to the neat and beautiful way in which Calvin presents the relationship between justification and sanctification, it may be that a good deal of this controversy would have been nipped in the bud. The nub of his thought is contained in the following words from his *Brief Confession of Faith.*

> I acknowledge that Jesus Christ not only justifies us by covering all our faults and sins, but also sanctifies us by his Spirit, so that the two things (the free forgiveness of sins and reformation to a holy life) cannot be dissevered and separated from each other.[1]

Calvin found the biblical basis of this in two Pauline teachings: first in the central place that he gives to union with Christ, the believer's identification with Christ in his death and resurrection and (prospectively) in his glorification (e.g. Romans 6). And then in the gifts that the ascended Christ provides for his people – wisdom, righteousness, sanctification and redemption.

> *Thirdly*, he (Paul) calls them our *sanctification*, by which he means, that we who are otherwise unholy by nature, are by his Spirit renewed unto holiness, that we may serve God. From this, also, we infer, that we cannot be justified freely through faith alone without at the same time living holily. For these fruits of grace are connected together, as it were, by an indissoluble tie, so that he who attempts to sever them does in a manner tear Christ in pieces.[2]

He presents the Pauline theme of union with Christ both as the source of the 'double grace' of reconciliation and sanctification and also as its means of delivery.

The two aspects of this one grace are, as the phrase 'double grace' implies, inseparably connected but conceptually distinct. The role that faith has in the reception of each of these graces underlines this. Justification, grounded in Christ's work, is received by faith, and sanctification comes through faith in God's promise and obedience to it. Justification is logically though not temporally prior to sanctification. So justification is not sanctification, nor is sanctification justification. A person's union with Christ begins in eternity and is personally realised in real time. It has a Trinitarian basis in the free cooperation of Father, Son and Spirit and is conveyed in time by the illuminating, energising and renovating work of Christ's Spirit. We do not receive this union by faith, but it is as a result of a prior eternal union that the Spirit begets faith in us. The Spirit draws to himself those given to him by the Father.[3] We can put the point more formally in terms of Calvin's Christology. As we noted in Chapter 4, for Calvin Christ is the one Mediator, the eternal Logos with a human nature. As the one Mediator, he has three distinct offices. As our Priest, he is our substitute through whom our sins are expiated, God's justice is satisfied and Christ's immaculate righteousness is reckoned to us. As our Prophet, he delivers God's word to us, the word which (among other things) clearly reveals the standard of right-living. And he is our King into whose kingdom we have been received. As Priest, Christ acts on behalf of us, whereas Christ's roles as Prophet and King have mainly to do with our subjective renewal, both individually and corporately. As members of his Christ's body, adopted into his family – Calvin majors on these New Testament analogies – we receive his word and he exercises his Prophetic and Kingly rule over us through his Spirit.

It is at this point in our treatment of Calvin that we begin to see how the central aspects of Christian theology that we have been considering – the Trinity, the Incarnation of Christ and the atonement – lead to true religion. There have already been hints of this: the God we are concerned with is a God 'as he is to us'; the knowledge of this God is not the sort of knowledge that flits in the brain but is accompanied by love, fear and obedience. In knowing God we come to know ourselves. In terms of our overall theological focus we are now moving from considering God the Father and God the Son to God the Holy Spirit. Calvin has been called the theologian of the Holy Spirit, and it is in this area that we can see Calvin's innovations or, as he believes, his recovery of the teaching of Christ and of the Apostles, particularly of Paul.

In his theology of the Holy Spirit Calvin is engaged in the dismantling of the mediaeval religious sacramental system – seven sacraments, each with *ex opere operato* efficacy in the hands of a priesthood. Coupled with this is an ethic of human merit in which some people may in various ways stockpile merits through which they are justified. Others might purchase from this stockpile.

Calvin is not merely engaged in a demolition-job, however. For he replaces this system with one in which the key elements are not sacramental efficacy through a human priesthood, but the efficacy of the Word in mind and will, promoted and made effective by Christ's Spirit. Priests offering the sacrifice of the Mass are replaced by ministers of the word of God, preachers and teachers of it (among whom Calvin was honoured to count himself). Human recipients of God's grace do not have merit, for their goodness, such as it is, is received from Christ, and even one's best efforts are tainted by sin and require forgiveness.

Through the ministry (in accordance with Christ's promise) the Holy Spirit through the Word brings men and women to *conversio*, to personal penitence, faith and obedience. Within the company of the faithful, the visible church, such piety is fed and enlivened by preaching and teaching, and by the two sacraments or Baptism and the Lord's Supper. These do not have a stand-alone value but have an efficacy only as they are understood through Scripture and received in faith.

This change can be seen clearly expressed in Calvin's view of the Christian ministry. Instead of a hierarchical system that was intrinsic to the Papacy, in which special grace is conferred through episcopal ordination, Calvin regards all Christian ministers as on a par. There are not several distinct 'orders', there is one order. This is expressed through the rule of the church through the presbytery, a peer group of ministers and elders who meet to order and govern the regional or local business of the church.

It is important to see that at the heart of the ecclesiastical abuses that Calvin (along with the other Reformers) sought to rectify are certain key claims, particularly the idea of justification by faith 'alone', as he (with Luther) insisted, and the impossibility of people meriting the favour of God. The Reformation was not simply the proposal and implementation of a set of administrative changes, a mere reorganisation, as administrators may restructure the Health Service or the Army. It has a precise intellectual basis drawn from Scripture: the nature of the ministry of Christ, and the consequent nature of the ministry of those who serve in his name. Calvin was consumed by the task of elaborating this basis.

This chapter attempts to follow him in this task. To do this we must take up where we left off at the end of Chapter 4, with the work of Christ and what he merited for men and women. When we have completed this task, we shall then go 'behind the scenes' and look at what Calvin believed was the basis of why we receive the unmerited grace of God, God's election of men and women in Christ and his predestinating of them to grace and glory.

HUMAN MERIT

To appreciate the priestly work of Christ, we must clearly understand Calvin's attitude to human merit. He is contemptuous of the very idea of human merit, and of the blindness of those who advocate it, even deploring the use of the term.

> I willingly abstain from disputes about words, but I could wish that Christian writers had always observed this soberness – that when there was no occasion for it, they had never thought of using terms foreign to the Scripture – terms which might produce much offence, but very little fruit. I ask, what need was there to introduce the word Merit, when the value of works might have been fully expressed by another term, and without offence?[4]

He is dismissive of the mediaeval idea that in order to be meritorious faith must be a free act, and that men and women are capable of acts of supererogation. Supererogation was at the heart of those abuses which so fired up Luther. Calvin breathes this air. He pours scorn on the idea of merit because he believes that it is entirely unscriptural and that it is at the heart of the religious abuses that were so clear a symptom of the church's error. It appears that the phrase 'creaturely merit' is for Calvin a contradiction in terms. To say that Calvin's disdains human merit purely for soteriological reasons misses the point.

His objection to human or angelic merit is rooted not in the nature of salvation, nor in the operations of an arbitrary divine will (which in any case he rejects, as we have seen), but in the metaphysics of creatureliness.[5] So it is not accurate to say that Calvin's objection to merit is merely nominal, and that agreement between him and his Roman Catholic foes could have been achieved by avoiding the word 'merit' and finding some other word or phrase, such as 'good works', even though Calvin would have preferred that phrase.

For Calvin no creature can be literally and truly self-righteous, because such a state would presuppose a creaturely source of righteousness that is independent of God. The angels show this to be impossible in that though the unfallen angels are impeccable, they do not have such impeccability *a se*, as is shown, according to Calvin, by the inherent instability of even the unfallen angels, they are liable to fall unless upheld by the power of Christ.[6]

So for Calvin there is no question of anyone in his own right meriting anything in the eyes of God. To say that someone merited something from God would mean that God was indebted to that person, that he had an obligation to reward her, which was for Calvin an unacceptable thought, as it also seems to have been for Aquinas.

Now it is clear that there is the greatest inequality between God and man; they are infinitely far from each other, and man's whole good is from God. Thus there can be no justice between man and God in the sense of an absolute equality, but only in the sense of a proportionate relationship, so far, that is to say, as each works in his own mode. Now the mode and measure of human capacity is set for man by God. And so man can only merit before God on the presupposition of the divine ordination, of such a kind that by his work and action man is to obtain from God as a sort of reward that for which God has allotted him a power of action.[7]

Had he not been in the midst of the Reformation conflict Calvin might have accepted such moderate language. But such statements, however carefully formulated, were both false to Scripture and irreligious. Even though Aquinas says that men and women can only merit something from God by his gift, and that man's whole power to do good is from God, nevertheless for Calvin the connotations of the unbiblical word 'merit' made it impossible to use. Like an inverted pyramid, the mediaeval system was based on the idea of merit; dislodge the apex and Calvin believed that the rest will tumble over. Fallen human nature, even with the 'assistance' of grace, was unable to merit anything. Men and women in Christ are *simul iustus et peccator*, at once righteous and sinful. Good acts are the result of the work of God's grace within us and even our best actions are tainted and so in need of God's forgiveness.[8]

As we noted in Chapter 4, this righteousness, the immaculate righteousness of Christ, is received by faith. Faith is not simply assent to the word of God, much less is it implicit belief in the teaching of the church. It is personal reliance upon the word of God. And it brings joy and peace, and assurance, in a way that the Roman doctrine of merit never could. The assurance of faith became one of the 'selling points' of the Reformation.

FAITH AND ASSURANCE

It is the function of faith to subscribe to God's truth whenever it is made known, and principally to rely upon Christ in his various offices. So faith involves belief in what God has said and is based upon the evidence that Scripture gives for itself that it is the Word of God. Faith contrasts with sight, not with reason. But it is more than belief, it is reliance, trust – here Calvin once more sounds the authentic Reformation note – in the promise of God. When it is fully formed such faith has the certainty that comes from recognising the authority of God himself; it is a form of knowledge. Such faith is the gift of the Spirit.

When he comes to offer a 'full definition' of faith, Calvin focuses more generally on God's benevolence.

We shall now have a full definition of faith if we say that it is a firm and sure knowledge (*firmam certamque cognitionem*) of the divine favour toward us, founded on the truth of a free promise in Christ, and revealed to our minds, and sealed on our hearts, by the Holy Spirit.[9]

But this definition of faith is not a definition in the sense of a set of necessary and sufficient conditions for the presence of faith to any degree. It is a definition of an ideal, of what faith ought to be like, of what at its best it is. This is clear from what he goes on to say.

On the one hand he stresses faith's certainty, yet before giving the definition of faith Calvin says that it is surrounded by error and unbelief, and after giving it he says that even weak faith is real faith. So there are degrees of faith, but to think of faith as required to reach a 'threshold' before it is effective would go against another Calvinian theme, that faith has a merely instrumental value. So the least faith is real faith.

One might compare having weak faith with coming across an obscure passage of Scripture. If a person doesn't know what that passage really means, how can he have faith in it, if faith implies knowledge? Calvin's answer is that in these cases the believer has implicit faith, faith (presumably) of the following form: whatever the true meaning of this obscure passage turns out to be, I will have faith in it.

We grant, indeed, that so long as we are pilgrims in the world faith is implicit, not only because as yet many things are hidden from us, but because, involved in the mists of error, we attain not to all.[10]

However, despite this recognition of the place of implicit faith Calvin is not in general well disposed to it, and he is emphatic (in his critique of the Roman view of implicit faith) that it is parasitic on the cases where faith is explicit. Writing about the first disciples he says,

But, although they gave credit to the words of one whom they knew to be true, yet the ignorance which still possessed their minds involved their faith in darkness, and left them in amazement. Hence they are said to have believed only when, by the reality, they perceive the truth of what Christ had spoken; not that they then began to believe, but the seed of a hidden faith, which lay as it were dead in their hearts, then burst forth in vigour. They had, therefore, a true but implicit faith, having reverently embraced Christ as the only teacher. Then, being taught by him, they felt assured that he was the author of salvation.[11]

And as regards weak faith,

Thus we see that a mind illumined with the knowledge of God is at first involved in much ignorance – ignorance, however, which is gradually removed. Still this partial ignorance or obscure discernment does not prevent that clear knowledge of the divine favour which holds the first and principal part in faith.[12]

So what Calvin is setting forth is not so much an empirical claim in the form of a reportive definition of faith, but an account of an ideal which is, by God's grace, attainable. Ideally, the internal testimony of the Holy Spirit brings utter certainty that Holy Scripture is the word of God. But prejudice and ignorance may get in the way, and in the presence of these obstacles the Spirit may convey faith that is less than ideal; assured faith coupled with doubt. So ideally, faith is assured faith, but it may in fact be accompanied by doubt, even as it may be weakened by presumption.

THE WILL AND CONVERSION

The second grace that Christ conveys to us is sanctification through Christ's Spirit so that 'we aspire to integrity and purity of life',[13] what in later Reformed theology came to be known simply as sanctification, but which Calvin (confusingly for us) sometimes refers to as *conversio*. *Conversio* for Calvin is not a once for all conversion experience, an event or series of events, like his own 'sudden conversion' or Augustine's conversion in the garden, which he recounts for us so movingly in his *Confessions*. Conversion in this, the more conventional sense, is for Calvin the beginning, or even merely the conscious beginning, of *conversio*, which embraces not only an initial turning to Christ from sin but also the process of life-long moral and spiritual renewal.

The key point to understanding Calvin's radical understanding of conversion, whether in its narrower sense or in *conversio*, the renewal of the moral and spiritual nature of a person, is that he held that as a result of the Fall the human race had lost free will. However, we must be careful here. Calvin did certainly not believe that the Fall had resulted in all people becoming robotic or in being fated to do what they did not want to do.

After the Fall our normal decision-making powers remain intact. We still have, as fallen people, beliefs and desires, plans and goals, and reason our way to achieving these, insofar as we are not thwarted by other factors, such as external pressure and outside circumstances over which we have no control. In all these respects we still enjoy free will. But as a result of the Fall we have lost the motivation to do what is right out of love of God and neighbour. So long as we are left to ourselves the power to regain such motivation is beyond us. The Reformers referred to this incapacity as the bondage or servitude of the will to sin.[14] Martin Luther wrote a book against Erasmus entitled *The Bondage of the Will*, and Calvin wrote one with a similar title *The Bondage and Liberation of the Will*, against the Roman Catholic theologian Albertus Pighius (c.1490–1542).[15] It is impossible to understand the theology of the Reformation, and Calvin's part in it, without recognising the Reformers' deep convictions about the effects of sin on human nature.

Why is this? Because such a view has implications for the idea of divine grace. If men and women are facing the wrong way, away from

God, and cannot turn themselves around, and do not want to turn themselves around, then the grace of God to them must be sufficiently strong to ensure the turning. It must be effective or 'efficacious' grace. To use the imagery of the New Testament, it must bring life to the dead, light to those in darkness. So the means that God uses must be 'alone effectual for their salvation'.[16] That is, God's grace must not only provide necessary conditions for conversion but also necessary *and sufficient* conditions. To confine God's grace to the provision of only necessary conditions would not be sufficient to break the chains. Besides, if it were, then this would imply that men and women have a natural, unaided power to cooperate with God's grace. Calvin believed that besides being unscriptural, such cooperation (which Augustine had emphatically rejected in his controversy with the Pelagians) lay at the heart of the mediaeval doctrine of human merit, the idea of works of supererogation, which we noted earlier. Calvin was greatly indebted to the anti-Pelagian writings of Augustine at such points. On one occasion he wrote that he would willingly formulate his own confession of faith using nothing but the words of Augustine.

Does the idea of effective or effectual grace mean that God forces himself on people? This question is based upon a misunderstanding. As Calvin saw things, in conversion God does not overpower people but renews their power to will what is good and God-glorifying. It is a serious misunderstanding of Calvin to suppose that for the human will the default position is a state of neutrality or equilibrium between evil and good. The default position is the willing obedience of God with which mankind was created. In the Fall mankind turned from God and became rebellious and disobedient – the new default position – and is restored only in conversion, as the Holy Spirit remakes and renews the will and men and women become, once more, willing lovers of the one true God.

They begin to regain the integrity of their original creation, their true humanity. This is the gift of Christ's atonement, the grace of being 'in Christ'. From it the particular virtues and graces of the Christian life flow, and with them the prospect of the recovery of the image of God in mankind. The graces flow gradually, for Calvin was not a perfectionist and he did not believe that at their first conversion men and women became thereafter incapable of sinning.

But Calvin notes that not all men and women are given such grace. He knew this from Scripture, from the choice of Abraham and the election of Israel, for example, and from what Paul teaches in Romans 8 and Ephesians 1, and also from empirical observation. Why do not all receive God's grace? This takes us into the thorny and mysterious region of divine election and predestination.

PREDESTINATION (AND PROVIDENCE)

We must now venture 'behind the scenes'. At one point in his treatment of justification Calvin writes as follows:

> The order of justification which it [Scripture] sets before us is this: first, God of his mere gratuitous goodness is pleased to embrace the sinner, in whom he sees nothing that can move him to mercy but wretchedness, because he sees him altogether naked and destitute of good works. He, therefore, seeks the cause of kindness in himself, that thus he may affect the sinner by a sense of his goodness, and induce him, in distrust of his own works, to cast himself entirely upon his mercy for salvation.[17]

Justification is not a reward for merit, nor do merits play any part in it. The same is true of sanctification, of *conversio*. As we have seen, it also has its source in God himself, Calvin says, and faith also plays a fundamental part here. The bestowing of the twofold graces of Christ's work is not random or haphazard, however, it has its 'reason' in God. By using such language Calvin takes us behind the scenes to God's secret choice, his election of the church, and his predestining of them to enjoy all the blessings of Christ's atonement, chief among which are justification and sanctification, leading to their glorification. Grace here and glory hereafter.

It would be a mistake to think that predestination, with which the name of Calvin is notoriously attached, is his invention, or that he was obsessed by it. Nor is predestination to be thought of as a 'central dogma' of Calvin's theology from which all other doctrines are derived or deduced. Calvin regarded himself as standing on the shoulders of the great doctors of the church – especially Augustine – and ultimately relying on the New Testament.

As we shall see, for Calvin predestination and providence are not easily separable, as if predestination has to do with God's grace, providence with 'nature', and as if a doctrine of providence is a piece of natural theology. Predestination is an aspect of divine providence.

(The fact that Calvin treats providence and predestination in different places in the 1559 edition of *Institutes* ought not to mislead us. Providence as he treats it in the *Institutes* is intertwined with the destiny of the church. I believe that he separated them, bringing providence forward to Book I, to minimise the potential for confusing free will as human choice, which is involved with providence, and free will as a well-motivated choice of the good, which is the result of predestination).

In the *Institutes* Calvin says that predestination is 'the eternal decree of God, by which he determined with himself whatever he wished to happen with regard to every man. All are not created on equal terms, but some are preordained to eternal life, others to eternal damnation.'[18]

However, it is important to grasp that although Calvin (and the classic Christian tradition) is not universalistic, even if he were a universalist, a doctrine of election and predestination would still be required. For as he saw things, whether viewed in particularistic or universalistic terms, salvation is not automatic. It is not a human right. It is willed by God, who need not have willed it. It is an utterly gracious act. So necessarily God has to make a choice, the choice to bring grace to men and women, and to destine those whom he chooses to faith and salvation through Christ, whether those whom he chooses are in fact the entire human race or only a part of it. The empirical fact that not everyone believes, together with the teaching of Scripture to that effect, leads Calvin to the conclusion that God's grace is not granted to the entire human race.

'Predestination' is often loosely thought of as equivalent to election and the destining of those elect to salvation. More exactly, predestination in the narrower sense is, Calvin says, the consequence of election. God chooses the church, his elect, by his pure grace and mercy and then predestines them to grace and glory through the means that he has provided. God is the author of predestination and, since God is eternal, predestination is eternal as well. So each person is born already destined to life or to death.

This is so-called 'double predestination', taught as clearly by Thomas Aquinas (say) as by John Calvin.[19] But it is also important to note that Calvin does not *deduce* reprobation from election; he does not argue that because some are predestined to life *therefore* some are predestined to death. Rather he finds reprobation clearly taught in Scripture and credible for that reason. (Calvin did not think that one ought to believe only what it is convenient or comfortable to believe, or what one can immediately fathom.) Further, while the destiny of each person is fixed before he or she is born, and God withholds his grace from some, those who suffer the fate of the reprobate do so because of their sin, which God has chosen to permit and mysteriously decreed (in their case) not to pardon. He passes them by, leaving them to the consequences of their own sin. Those who are elected are not, in a symmetrical way, elected because of their merit (as we have already seen, Calvin abhors that idea) but solely as a result of God's grace, coming to them in a way that is utterly undeserved.

Though the 'passing over' is due only to God's will, nevertheless the ground of condemnation of those passed over lies in their own guilt. 'Though their perdition depends upon the predestination of God, the cause and matter of it is in themselves.'[20] Why are those who are elected favoured over those who are reprobated? Those who ask this question 'will in vain torment themselves in seeking for a deeper cause than the secret and inscrutable counsel of God'.[21] The God who reprobates is not God of 'absolute might'. For 'the will of God is not only free from all vice but is the supreme standard of perfection, the law of all laws.'[22]

So there is a significant asymmetry between election (and the subsequent predestination to glory) and reprobation (predestination to judgment), which the phrase 'double predestination' (which is not Calvin's language) does not capture.

Calvin also distinguishes between the election of the nation of Israel and that of individuals.

Although it is now sufficiently plain that God by his secret counsel chooses whom he will while he rejects others, his gratuitous election has only been partially explained until we come to the case of single individuals, to whom God not only offers salvation, but so assigns it, that the certainty of the result remains not dubious or suspended. These are considered as belonging to that one seed of which Paul makes mention (Rom. 9.8; Gal 3.16, etc.). For although adoption was deposited in the hand of Abraham, yet as many of his posterity were cut off as rotten members, in order that election may stand and be effectual, it is necessary to ascend to the head in whom the heavenly Father hath connected his elect with each other, and bound them to himself by an indissoluble tie.[23]

Not only is God the author of predestination, he is also the source of it. Calvin is emphatic that those who are predestined do not depend upon anything in them that God foreknows and that qualifies them to receive his mercy. As he puts it, commenting on Romans 8.29, the foreknowledge of God 'is not a bare prescience . . . but the adoption by which he had always distinguished his children from the reprobate'. And again in his comment on Romans 11.2 ('God has not rejected his people whom he foreknew'), Calvin says,

> by the verb *foreknow* is not to be understood a foresight, I know not of what, by which God foresees what sort of being any one will be, but that good pleasure, according to which he has chosen those as sons to himself, who, being not yet born, could not have procured for themselves his favour.[24]

These are the remnant, chosen by grace (v.5).

Unconditional election and the predestination that accompanies it raise obvious objections. The election of some and the passing by of others seems quite unfair. And the basis on which the election is grounded, since it cannot be for merit in the ones chosen or indeed anything that would predispose God to favour them, seems arbitrary. How does Calvin answer these points?

It is important to understand that Calvin is not a philosopher, handling inert data, concepts and arguments. He is confronted by the announcement of the will of the sovereign Creator and Redeemer. Whatever may be said to reduce the starkness of unconditional election, it is ultimately a matter of the character of God's purpose. The regress of explanation is not stopped by a brute empirical fact, or by the operation of luck or chance or fate, but with the righteous will of God.

God's will is not arbitrary, nevertheless his reason is hidden. On this Calvin is emphatic.

> The will of God is the supreme rule of righteousness, so that everything which he wills must be held to be righteous by the mere fact of his willing it. Therefore, when it is asked why the Lord did so, we must answer, Because he pleased. But if you proceed farther to ask why he pleased, you ask for something greater and more sublime than the will of God, and nothing such can be found. . . .
> We, however, give no countenance to the fiction of absolute power,

which, as it is heathenish, so it ought to be held in detestation by us. We do not imagine God to be lawless. He is a law to himself . . . the will of God is not only free from all vice, but is the supreme standard of perfection, the law of all laws.[25]

That is one answer: God's will is righteous, but inscrutable. 'We must always return to the mere pleasure of the divine will, the cause of which is hidden in himself.'[26] But, of course, this is not an answer to the objection. It simply locates the place where the answer is to be found.

But why, if some are chosen to eternal life, do others perish? Calvin's answer to this question is to argue that God does not owe anything to any person and so has no obligations to treat everyone equally.

As we are all vitiated by sin, we cannot but be hateful to God, and that not from tyrannical cruelty, but the strictest justice. But if all whom the Lord predestines to death are naturally liable to sentence of death, of what injustice, pray, do they complain? . . . Hence it appears how perverse is this affectation of murmuring, when of set purpose they suppress the cause of condemnation which they are compelled to recognise in themselves, that they may lay the blame upon God.[27]

Summarising, there is a sense in which Calvin's attitude to these problems is religious, not philosophical. In our effort to discover the rationale for God's action we come to the limits of human comprehension. We can note certain features of God's action, but ultimately we must recognise God's sovereignty and especially his righteousness, and reverence both. So Calvin is guarded and careful in the way in which he approaches the 'secret' purposes of God. But he is not embarrassed. He thinks that the teaching of predestination has positive value. It underlines the freeness of God's grace and humbles the believer, while at the same time making him confident about the future.

PROVIDENCE

As we have said, for Calvin predestination is an aspect of providence. According to him, God not only created the universe, he also rules or governs every aspect of it, including evil events and actions. And he rules the created order teleologically, in order to accomplish a certain end or ends. Those events that are evil and that apparently thwart his will are in fact made to serve his will; God 'willingly permits' evil and so all actions, including evil actions, are decreed by him. The language of willing permission, which Calvin borrowed from Augustine, is meant to show that God decrees the evil, but not in the sense that he is himself morally culpable. In some sense God wills the evil; he does not exercise merely a general providential supervision. Calvin thought that the idea of a mere general supervision, besides being unscriptural, came dangerously near to the idle deity of the Epicureans. God's providence is thus all-embracing.

> For whoso has learned from the mouth of Christ that all the hairs of his head are numbered (Matt. 10.30), will look farther for the cause, and hold that all events whatsoever are governed by the secret counsel of God.[28]

In defending such a comprehensive account of providence, Calvin was not introducing a novelty into the Christian faith, even though his account of providence is perhaps unmatched in its clarity and trenchancy. His view was simply the standard Christian view. Thomas Aquinas affirms that everything is subject to divine providence.

> Now the causality of God, who is the first efficient cause, covers all existing things, immortal and mortal alike, and not only their specific principles but also the source of their singularity. Hence everything that is real in any way whatsoever is bound to be directed by God to an end; as the Apostle remarks, *The things that are of God are well-ordered.* (Rom. 13.1). Since his Providence is naught else than the idea whereby all things are planned to an end, as we have said, we conclude quite strictly that all things in so far as they are real come under divine Providence.[29]

For Calvin predestination is that aspect of God's governance of all things that concerns the destiny of the elect and of the reprobate. Even when he separated providence from predestination in his ordering of material in the *Institutes*, the examples he uses in discussing how providence works are often drawn from the affairs of the church, both from the Old Testament and New Testament. For Calvin claims that all events are governed by God's secret plan, especially those that concern his church, and that nothing takes place without his deliberation. God so attends the regulation of individual events, and they all so proceed from his set plan, that nothing takes place by chance. God has a special care for his church, and in any case it is only the believer who can make the proper use of the doctrine of providence. Predestination, then, is implied not only by the doctrine of providence itself but also by the proper use of that doctrine.

Hence, our Saviour, after declaring that even a sparrow falls not to the ground without the will of his Father, immediately makes the application, that being more valuable than many sparrows, we ought to consider that God provides more carefully for us. He even extends this so far, as to assure us that the hairs of our head are all numbered. What more can we wish, if not even a hair of our head can fall, save in accordance with his will? I speak not merely of the human race in general. God having chosen the Church for his abode, there cannot be a doubt, that in governing it, he gives singular manifestations of his paternal care.[30]

It is a linchpin of Calvin's account of the relation of providence and evil that there is 'diversity of purpose' in providence; in the one event, a human agent, Satan and the Lord may each have different purposes. He works this out in some detail.

How can we attribute the same work to God, to Satan, and to man, without either excusing Satan by the interference of God, or making God the author of the crime? This is easily done, if we look first to the end, and then to the mode of acting. The Lord designs to exercise the patience of his servant by adversity; Satan's plan is to drive him to despair; while the Chaldeans are bent on making unlawful gain by plunder. Such diversity of purpose makes a wide distinction in the act. In the mode there is not less difference. The Lord permits Satan to afflict his servant; and the Chaldeans, who had been chosen as the ministers to execute the deed, he hands over to the impulses of Satan, who, pricking on the already depraved Chaldeans with his poisoned darts, instigates them to commit the crime. They rush furiously on to the unrighteous deed, and become its guilty perpetrators. Here Satan is properly said to act in the reprobate, over whom he exercises his sway, which is that of wickedness. God also is said to act in his own way; because even Satan, when he is the instrument of divine wrath, is completely under the command of God, who turns him as he will in the execution of his just judgments.[31]

Furthermore, 'the several kinds of things are moved by a secret impulse of nature', though Calvin emphasises that God is the origin and the immediate sustainer of all that there is.

While God is the first cause and the upholder of all that he has created and his governance of the universe is not enclosed 'within the stream of nature' nor borne along by a 'universal law of nature', nevertheless different kinds of secondary causes operate in the creation. Calvin is not an occasionalist; he does not think that there is only one causal agent in the entire universe, God, and all other so-called causes as simply constant conjunctions of events. Nor does this emphasis on sovereignty indicate a mechanistic outlook because, as we have noted, divine providence is a teleological arrangement for Calvin. So there is an enormous difference between providence and fatalism or physical determinism. The natural ends of the various orders of creation may be thought of as subordinated to the ultimate divine end. Calvin carefully attempts to balance an emphasis upon divine sovereignty with a recognition of secondary causes of various kinds. We shall consider Calvin's practical application of the idea of providence in Chapter 6.

CHRIST AS THE MIRROR OF ELECTION

Earlier we discussed Calvin's attitude to the assurance of faith. We may now consider this from another perspective. Granted that Calvin holds that not everyone is elected by God to salvation and so predestined by him to grace and glory, the question arises: how may a person know whether or not he is among the chosen?

In a classic passage in the *Institutes* Calvin asserts that Jesus Christ is the mirror of our election. Calvin explicitly guards himself against the charge that the particularism of eternal election ought to lead to speculation and uncertainty as to whether we are among the elect. To avoid self-deception we must reason from our communion with Christ.

But if we are elected in him, we cannot find the certainty of our election in ourselves; and not even in God the Father, if we look at him apart from the Son. Christ, then is the mirror in which we ought, and in which, without deception, we may contemplate our election. For since it is into his body that the Father has decreed to ingraft those whom from eternity he wished to be his, that he may regard as sons all whom he acknowledges to be his members, if we are in communion with Christ, we have proof sufficiently clear and strong that we are written in the Book of Life.[32]

In interpreting Calvin the influential twentieth-century theologian Karl Barth seemed to think that his use of the idea of a 'mirror' is simply a strategy, a pastoral rule for changing the subject from the *decretum absolutum* to Christ.[33] But this is not so. According to Calvin, God's decree to save some particular person cannot now be separated from all the means that he has also decreed to bring that person to *conversio* and to his final destiny. Perhaps God could have decreed another set of means. For example, perhaps he could have decreed that on being converted a person should be immediately translated to heaven, thus avoiding a long and often wearisome earthly pilgrimage. But (Calvin thinks) it is profitless to speculate on what might have been. We can only find the certainty of our election in Christ. He is the mirror of election; that is, it is a person's relation to Christ, or rather the evidence of that relation, that gives her the only possible grounds to be assured that she is indeed a Christian. She has no other means open to her, least of all the means of having direct access to God's mind to discern whom he has eternally elected. Calvin's point is a logical one and thus a point of principle. It is not merely pragmatic or pedagogic.

This is one answer to those troubled by the thought that predestination makes us helpless. The chief thing, for Calvin, is that a person should be in communion with Christ. If a person comes to Christ, enjoying his twofold grace, then as far as Calvin is concerned that person is entitled to draw the inference that he is elected.

Without question, the matters we have been touching on are both difficult to follow and difficult to swallow. Calvin does not deny this. But as the last phase of our discussion has shown, he nevertheless has a very practical view of how these abstruse matters are to work themselves out. Predestination is not simply a theological conundrum, something for the professionals. The fact of predestination is not to be a source of speculation, but to encourage us to be sure of our relation to Christ, the mirror of election. Calvin's teaching on

God's grace in Christ, and his providential governing of all events, is intended to enrich and to give character to our lives. The fact of *God's* providence over all things is to energise us to use the means he has provided for the present, and to do our best to prepare for the future, while leaving the outcome in his hands. We'll look at such matters in more detail in Chapter 6.

CHAPTER 6

THE CHRISTIAN LIFE

We have seen that, according to Calvin, by his atonement Christ procured a double grace, justification, the reckoning of a person righteous, appropriated by faith only, and sanctification, the setting apart of that person for the knowledge and service of God which brings about life-long renewal, the life of faith. The two gifts are distinct but inseparable. The way in which this double grace is distributed has its origin in God's eternal election.

In this chapter we pursue Calvin's understanding of how the Christian life is to be lived. Christ as Prophet gives his people his Word to live by, and faith to put it into practice, and as their King he rules them. But we see his kingly work more particularly in his rule of society, and of the Christian church within it, to which we shall come in Chapter 7.

THE SPRINGS OF ACTION

Like his hero Augustine, John Calvin places enormous stress upon motive and intention in human action. The Fall means that men and women serve the creature rather than their Creator. God's grace in Christ, and especially the idea of the believer's union with Christ, reverse this. The stance of the Christian life in all its aspects, but especially in its ethical aspect, is responsive. It is a response to what Christ has done, and so it is to be marked by love, gratitude and service. Calvin was insistent that the Reformation doctrine of justification by faith alone was not antinomian. His idea of Christ's double grace, two distinct and yet inseparable blessings, brilliantly ensures this. At every turn he distanced himself from the 'Libertines', an umbrella term for various radical groups who were antinomian, believing either in some form of perfectionism or inferring from the believers' new status in Christ that they are 'free from the law' as a rule of conduct. In Calvin this anti-antinomian emphasis expresses itself in a rather startling way. In Book III of the *Institutes* he discusses the nature, characteristics and ethical standard of the Christian life *before* he discusses justification by faith alone. By structuring his discussion in this fashion Calvin makes it as clear as can be that union with Christ has essential moral implications.

He makes a basic distinction between the rule of living and the motive(s) for it.[1] In this section we shall consider what Calvin has to say about the inner springs of action.

For you cannot divide the matter with God, undertaking part of what his word enjoins, and omitting part at pleasure. For, in the first place, God uniformly recommends integrity as the principal part of his worship, meaning by integrity real singleness of mind, devoid of gloss and fiction, and to this is opposed a double mind; as if it had been said, that the spiritual commencement of a good life is when the internal affections are sincerely devoted to God, in the cultivation of holiness and justice.[2]

The believer is in union with God. By these expressions 'union with God' and 'union with Christ', Calvin does not intend a kind of divinisation of the human person, or anything which implies a loss of identity or individuality, a merging of the human with the divine. On the other hand, the identification reaches beyond mere fellow-feeling. It is an identification of a person's spirit and intent with Christ's own spirit, arising from the fact that he has been given to Christ, follows him in death and resurrection, and is a member of his body. So it is a sharing in the concreteness of Christ's ministry, not of course in the sense of being a co-redeemer (that's a blasphemous idea, for Calvin), or in metaphysical union with Christ, but in the sense that the person benefits from Christ's work through close and exclusive identification with Christ in his work. 'Mystical' is the term often used for this union, but it is not very informative.

Such union is thus the closest kind of association, of feeling and affection, of mutual sympathy and aim and goal. One so united is therefore identified with God, and he is not to 'think, speak, design, or act, without a view to his glory',[3] and so to deny his old (and remaining) sinful self.

In elaborating this Calvin keeps up a continuous polemic against 'the philosophers', though he does not identify any of them by name. There are various elements to his critique: the philosophers teach that we should follow our nature (no doubt he has the Stoics in mind here). The trouble is that they have no conception of the fallenness of human nature.

Come, then, and let them show me a more excellent system among philosophers, who think that they only have a moral philosophy duly and orderly arranged. They, when they would give excellent exhortations to virtue, can only tell us to live agreeably to nature. Scripture derives its exhortations from the true source, when it not only enjoins us to regulate our lives with a view to God its author to whom it belongs; but after showing us that we have degenerated from our true origin – viz. the law of our Creator, adds, that Christ, through whom we have returned to favour with God, is set before us as a model, the image of which our lives should express.[4]

Detailing this, Calvin adds, 'These, I say, are the surest foundations of a well-regulated life, and you will search in vain for anything resembling them among philosophers who, in their commendation of virtue, never rise higher than the natural dignity of man'. As part of this mistake, the philosophers think that our reason is sufficient to motivate us.

They give the government of man to reason alone, thinking that she alone is to be listened to; in short, they assign to her the sole direction of the conduct. But Christian philosophy bids her give place, and yield complete submission to the Holy Spirit, so that the man himself no longer lives, but Christ lives and reigns in him (Gal. 2.20).[5]

Though he stresses the 'inwardness' of the Christian life, and its distinctiveness, Calvin does not think that he is insisting upon unattainable counsels of perfection. People must begin from where they are. Furthermore, even the most successful efforts are tarnished. Calvin's polemic against merit surfaces again at this point. Since our best efforts are, in God's eyes, still affected by sin, what chance is there of accumulating a reserve of merit? So there is need for the believer to continue to pray, 'Forgive us our trespasses'.

But seeing that, in this earthly prison of the body, no man is supplied with strength sufficient to hasten in his course with due alacrity, while the greater number are so oppressed with weakness, that hesitating, and halting, and even crawling on the ground they make little progress, let every one of us go as far as his humble ability enables him, and prosecute the journey once begun.[6]

Perhaps Calvin has his own irritability and excitability in mind here, exacerbated as these were by his frequent migraines and fevers. So the Christian life is marked by dedication and devotion to God, following the example of Christ. But such self-denial is not a romantic, sentimentalised, following of Jesus, as Calvin makes clear in the following passage. Commenting on Titus 2:11–14 he says,

After holding forth the grace of God to animate us, and pave the way for His true worship, he removes the two greatest obstacles stand in the way, viz. ungodliness, to which we are by nature too prone, and worldly lusts, which are of still greater extent. . . . Thus he enjoins us, in regard to both tables of the Law, to lay aside our own mind, and renounce whatever our own reason and will dictate.[7]

To understand Calvin here we must, then, distinguish between motive and moral standard. The motive, as we have seen, is deeply and characteristically Christian: gratitude to God for our union with Christ and, taking him as our example, self-denial. But what then are we to do? How are we to live?

Calvin's answer is clear. It is the Moral Law, given to Moses and endorsed by Christ, which is to provide the standard of right living. This emphasis on the Law as the rule of life, the so-called 'third use' of the Law (besides its use to restrain evil, and its use to show us our own need and to call us to repentance on account of our failure), came to be characteristic of the Reformed (as against the Lutheran) wing of the Reformation.

WHAT IS VALUABLE?

While as we have seen Calvin stresses the non-natural, even supernatural character of Christian motivation, the rule of life, the moral standard, is rooted in the nature of things. Despite his stress on divine sovereignty Calvin is not a divine command theorist. He does not think that something is morally good simply because God commands it; at least, not as far as the two Tables of the Moral Law are concerned. He regarded 'What if?' questions ('What if God were to permit adultery?') as blasphemous.

So the moral law now no longer condemns us, because Christ has fulfilled the law on our behalf and whose righteousness is reckoned to us. It is an expression of 'eternal law' or 'natural law'. (He seems, on the few occasions when he uses these expressions, to do so interchangeably.) This law has an abiding, central place in the flourishing of human life.

It is true that Calvin recognises that there is one contingent, or at least a time-conditioned feature of the first Table of the law, namely the command regarding Sabbath observance. But (with the exception of the Sabbath) Calvin uses language that points to the non-contingent character of the second Table. Thus in his prefatory remarks on the Decalogue he writes of the law that has been handed down to us to teach us perfect righteousness,[8] and that the two Tables contain 'a complete rule of righteousness'.[9] Further, in his discussion of the division of the law into two Tables there is no suggestion that between the two there is a difference in their ethical character. Finally, Calvin sees the Decalogue as a spelling out the standard of that one law; 'the very things contained in the two tables are, in a manner, dictated to us by that internal law which . . . is in a manner written and stamped on every heart'.[10] So the moral law reproduces natural law, in clear senses of 'natural' – what is innate, original and universal.

This emphasis does not mean that Calvin completely disconnects the command of God from moral obligation. For he holds that God's command is sufficient for *knowing* what we ought to do. But it is not necessary for such knowledge because we already have a more general though more inchoate guide to the divine will, besides God's explicit command, an innate awareness of natural law and the possession of a sense of equity. So that God's command sharpens that understanding of what we ought to do that is derived from such sources. It follows that for Calvin the divine commands chiefly have an epistemic role. They tell us in clear terms what our duty is, and their force as imperatives highlights our obligations.[11] So while what God commands underlines the deliverances of the natural law and of our general sense of equity, it does not supplant these.

CALVIN AND NATURAL LAW

If the Decalogue reflects what is 'natural' what is Calvin's attitude to natural law? As we noted in Chapter 1, there has been a strong tendency among some interpreters of Calvin and of the Reformed tradition, starting with Kuyper and Bavinck, to see Calvin's views about ethics, and particularly about the ethical capacities of those who are outside the church, in terms of the operation of 'common grace'. Such interpreters have drawn an opposition between such grace and natural law, for they believe that Calvin rejected natural law as part of his critique of the nature–grace thinking of mediaevalism.

'Nature' thus understood is regarded by the defenders of common grace as an area of human life which is autonomous, self-propelled and morally pure, an area where God and his grace are unnecessary. On such a view divine grace is said to presuppose and build on nature, not to supplant it. Rejecting (on behalf of Calvin) this relation of nature and grace as operating on two levels, the upholders of the 'common grace' view argue that the whole of life is so infected and skewed by sin that the restraining and gifting of God are not to be explained in terms of the workings of nature, but they are the result of God's 'common' or 'general', that is, non-saving, grace.

But Calvin, the Calvin of the *Institutes* rather than the Calvin of later tradition, would have been quite puzzled by such a presentation of his ideas. There is the question of whether he would have recognised the view of Aquinas and mediaevalism adopted by later Calvinists as authentic. Furthermore, he himself showed no signs of making such a sharp opposition between 'nature' and 'common grace'. Natural law and the sense of equity on which it is based are both regarded as the gifts of God. Their reception is infected by sin, nevertheless they continue to be effective as a result of God's undeserved goodness, and so are his 'gracious' provision. When as part of the original gift of the divine image God imbued men and women with a recognition of the law, this was a gift to them. Though affected by sin, the gift remains. In giving or not withdrawing these gifts God restrains the potential effects of sin and provides the basis on which tolerable lives can be lived and human culture can flourish.

So Calvin's attitude to natural law is by no means negative or dismissive. He does not draw attention to natural law and equity simply to eliminate them; rather he has a positive view of them. Nor is he using 'natural law' in a way that equivocates on the scholastic use.

Rather there are several significant points of similarity (as well as points of difference) with, for example, Thomas Aquinas's usage. The main difference is that Calvin has a dimmer view of the powers of fallen mankind to discern its duty from the natural law and to be motivated to do it. So the difference between Calvin and his mediaeval forbears is one of degree rather than one of principle.

> In every age there have been some who, under the guidance of nature, were all their lives devoted to virtue. It is of no consequence, that many blots may be detected in their conduct; by the mere study of virtue, they evinced that there was somewhat of purity in their nature. . . . Such examples, then, seem to warn us against supposing that the nature of man is utterly vicious, since, under its guidance, some have not only excelled in illustrious deeds, but conducted themselves most honourably through the whole course of their lives. But we ought to consider, that, notwithstanding of the corruption of our nature, there is some room for divine grace, such grace as, without purifying it, may lay it under internal restraint.[12]

God's grace may restrain the corruption of nature without regenerating it.

For Calvin natural law seems to have three essential features. It sets out certain values rooted in human nature and in its God-given end. Second, the law is known to us all and recognised as obligatory without reliance upon God's special revelation. Third, the law is not restricted to a particular culture or epoch, but applies to everyone everywhere. As we have seen, Calvin thinks that the social aspect of the natural law has a rough correspondence with the Second Table of the Decalogue in the sense that societies arrive at such laws governing the family, truth-telling and property, for example, unaided by special revelation. Most strikingly of all, perhaps, there are places where he equates natural law with the Golden Rule. Here are two references from his *Sermons on the Ten Commandments*. When discussing theft, he says,

> Furthermore, seeing that we should not operate in such a way by either finesse or subtlety, it is crucial for us to return to that natural law, (*equité naturelle*) which is, that we ought to do unto others as we want them to do unto us. When we follow that rule, it

is unnecessary to have thick tomes in order to learn not to steal, for, in brief, everyone knows how he ought to walk with his fellow man, that is, that he should not harbor malice, or attempt to enrich himself at his neighbor's expense, or gain for himself substance which is not his own.[13]

Later in these *Sermons* there is a reference to the natural law of not doing anything to anyone unless we would want them to do the same to us.[14]

Without being aware of Jesus' teaching, everyone knows what the Golden Rule teaches. So the law of nature is that law of God which concerns the relationships of people with each other. It is known to some degree by all human beings, for even 'barbarians' are not as barbaric as could be. Yet Calvin is also clear that due to sin humankind is unable by the exercise of its own powers alone (action that is 'natural' in yet another sense) to reacquire and retain the knowledge of God's natural law in its entirety. Nevertheless he adds that through the continued activity of conscience each person knows enough of God's original, natural law, as a result of which he is rendered inexcusable before God for his sin.

In his *Commentary* on Romans 2.15 he says that there is not in men a full knowledge of the law, only some seeds of what is right implanted in their nature, some notions of justice and rectitude. Yet these seeds grew and blossomed. All nations 'of themselves and without a monitor, are disposed to make laws for themselves', they have laws to punish adultery, and theft and murder, and they commend good faith in contracts. So the seed of religion that remains in fallen human nature has a moral dimension. It does not remain dormant but expresses itself in laws that fairly closely shadow the laws of the Decalogue. The recognition of natural obligations apart from revelation exercises a restraining influence.

Nevertheless we have already noted that for Calvin some parts of the Decalogue are related to an earlier economy of divine revelation. Writing about the Fourth Commandment Calvin distinguishes between those features of it which are ceremonial from those that are moral (and hence in some sense natural). By Christ's coming the ceremonial part of the commandment to remember the Sabbath day to keep it holy was abolished (implying that the non-ceremonial part of it was not).

For Calvin the Lord's Day of the New Testament is inextricably bound up with the fact of Christ's resurrection. So perhaps we can say that while the law of nature, in Calvin's view, obliges all men to keep days of rest, and perhaps obliges them to keep the seventh day (in Calvin's commentary on Genesis the seventh-day Sabbath is regarded as a 'creation ordinance'),[15] it does not oblige all men everywhere and at all times to keep the seventh day as the Sabbath as Jews under Moses were commanded to do.

Laws which flout the second Table of the moral law are *ipso facto* inequitable, and so we should not exaggerate the pluralism that may seem to be implicit in what Calvin sometimes says. The point is that different systems of laws may express the same values, even the same basic laws, in different ways, perhaps through imposing varying kinds of rewards and punishments. So long as they express the moral law fairly they are to be approved. Calvin's conviction that it is the duty of the magistrate to uphold the moral law is clearly in evidence here. We shall consider its significance in Chapter 7.

LIBERTY, LUXURY, CALLING

We have already noted that for Calvin, although ethics is grounded in nature and known through conscience, its clarification and supplementation through special revelation is in the form of a set of commands. These commands, both in the form of the Decalogue and in the Golden Rule as taught by Jesus, have a kind of representative character. So the command to honour one's father and mother is not restricted in scope to one's parents but is concerned with family relationships, and duties to the elderly, more generally. One might think that this habit of extending the boundaries of the law, coupled with Calvin's intense belief that everything should be done for the glory of God, would mean that no area of life falls outside the scope of divine law in some way or other. The law maps out areas of obligation; it does not specify the boundaries of our obligation.

But it would be a mistake to conclude this. For while everything a Christian does ought to be done for the glory of God, not everything that a person may do is either commanded or forbidden by God. There are areas of life that are, as far as the law of God is concerned, 'indifferent', in which no particular action is commanded or forbidden, but where types of action are permitted. In these areas the Christian has liberty.

There is a Reformation principle at stake here: to go where Scripture leads and to go no further, to 'the very dangerous thing of binding consciences in closer fetters than those in which they are bound by the word of God'.[16]

Part of Calvin's polemic against the Roman Church is that it has passed laws to place restraint upon the conscience. This is unlawful: 'Our consciences have not to do with men but with God only'.[17] The laws enacted by the Roman Church, and by the magistrate in alliance with church, illegitimately reach into areas where there is liberty of conscience.

> The pretext, then, on which our false bishops burden the conscience with new laws is, that the Lord has constituted them spiritual legislators, and given them the government of the Church. Hence they maintain that everything which they order and prescribe must, of necessity, be observed by the Christian people.[18]

But Calvin says,

> They are not at all entitled to insist that whatever they devise without authority from the word of God shall be observed by the Church as matter of necessity. Since such power was unknown to the apostles, and was so often denied to the ministers of the Church by our Lord himself, I wonder how any have dared to usurp, and dare in the present day to defend it, without any precedent from the apostles, and against the manifest prohibition of God.[19]

This freedom that people innately possess against unwarranted government by the leadership of the church is an instance of a general principle: whatever is neither commanded nor forbidden by God is permitted by him and may be done to his own glory. This category of the 'morally indifferent' permits the cultivation of personal space.

However, we must neither think of it as liberty in the modern liberal sense nor as involving or even implying participatory democracy. Further, it is quite anachronistic to suppose that in his teaching on Christian liberty Calvin is consciously mapping out a path that will lead to modern views of personal liberty and human rights. Nevertheless, Calvin's underlying principle that neither the magistrate nor the church, acting illegitimately as a magistrate, has the right to command or permit what God has forbidden or to forbid what God has commanded or permitted, is of considerable significance.

The idea of the morally indifferent, and the moral space it permits, is augmented by what Calvin has to say about the enjoyment of God's gifts to us. It is going beyond Scripture to require people to restrict what they eat or wear to what is strictly necessary for their survival. How are we to use these gifts? What should be our attitude to them?

Calvin's general response is: the safe guide to thinking about the use of such gifts is to answer the question, What is God's purpose in giving them to us? Why, for example, does he give us food and clothing? His answer is surprisingly generous.

> Let this be our principle, that we err not in the use of the gifts of Providence when we refer them to the end for which their author made and destined them, since he created them for our good, and nor for our destruction . . . he consulted not only for our necessity, but also for our enjoyment and delight. Thus, in clothing, the end was, in addition to necessity, comeliness and honour; and in herbs, fruits and trees, besides their various uses, gracefulness of appearance and sweetness of smell. . . . Has the Lord adorned flowers with all the beauty which spontaneously presents itself to the eye, and the sweet odour which delights the sense of smell, and shall it be unlawful for us to enjoy that beauty and this odour? What? Has he not so distinguished colours as to make some more agreeable than others? Has he not given qualities to gold and silver, ivory and marble, thereby rendering them precious above other metals or stones? In short, has he not given many things a value without having any necessary use?[20]

Early on in his writings, in the first edition of the *Institutes* in 1536 he writes eloquently and amusingly against a cramped, narrow, legalistic frame of mind with respect to what is permitted.

> If someone begins to doubt whether it is lawful for him to use linen for his sheets or shirts or handkerchiefs or serviettes, he will go on to become uncertain about hessian and at last be doubtful about using even canvas. For he will think to himself 'Could I not eat my meals without a serviette? Do I really need to carry a handkerchief?' If it should occur to a man that some rather pleasant

food was unlawful, he will get to the point of not being able to eat black bread or common dishes without an uneasy conscience before God, for it will occur to him that he could nourish his body on food yet more humble. If he is doubtful about a fairly good wine, he will then not be able to drink some rot-gut with a good conscience, and in the end he will dare touch no water that is sweeter and purer than usual. And at last such a man will think it a sin to step over a straw on the path, as they say.[21]

Condemning such scruples clearly goes some way beyond Calvin's objections to the church's imposition of her own man-made rules.

There are, Calvin says, two main rules of guidance in this area, rules arising from the Gospel rather than from the Law. The first is that the Christian must always recognise that he is on a pilgrimage to a heavenly city. [I Cor. 7. 29–31]. The second rule is that 'we must learn to be no less placid and patient in enduring penury, than moderate in enjoying abundance'.[22] He recommends an attitude of personal detachment arising from our Christian walk rather than the imposition of more rules.

Calvin adds a third principle:

[Earthly blessings] have all been given us by the kindness of God, and appointed for our use under the condition of being regarded as trusts, of which we must one day give account. We must, therefore, administer them as if we constantly heard the words sounding in our ears, 'Give an account of your stewardship'.[23]

We shall return to these themes in the last section.

Another noteworthy feature of Calvin's approach to ethics is that even where the law of God reaches us, and we refrain from doing what the law forbids, he does not to seek to apply the law casuistically, or tie every aspect of behaviour to a 'strict rule'.[24] He deliberately turns away from settling moral problems by adjudication between rival moral authorities and instead writes that 'consciences neither can nor ought to be bound by fixed and definite laws; but that Scripture having laid down general rules for the legitimate use, we should keep within the limits they prescribe'.[25] He does not approach moral problems by identifying many distinct 'cases of conscience', which may be endlessly argued over, but in terms of the spirit behind the law rather than its letter. It is altogether outside Calvin's mentality to give advice about ethical problems by finding an approach by which the letter of the law may be observed while its intent is ignored. We have seen this already in his view that the application of the law is to be governed by the principle of equity.

However, here are two exceptions to this general approach to ethics. One is the issue of 'Nicodemism'. Calvin was bombarded with questions from evangelicals in France as to whether (like Nicodemus, the ruler of the Jews, who came to Jesus by night (John 3.1–2)) they should disguise their faith in the hope that the evangelical cause might grow as an 'underground church'. Calvin's response to such difficult issues is always unequivocal. While the believers in France ought to do nothing to antagonise the authorities by flaunting their faith, and while in many cases flight from France to Geneva or Zurich or to some other Protestant city would be the preferred option, they should, while remaining in France, never deny their faith by, for example, attending and participating in the Mass. He laid out his position in his *On Shunning the Unlawful Rites of the Ungodly* (1537)[26] and later in *Apology to the Nicodemites* (1544) as well as in many letters written in response to the unfavourable reactions to his advice. For Calvin, Nicodemism was a clear flouting of the Apostolic principle that we ought to obey God rather than men.

The second area of exception is the reform of Genevan law. As part of the Reformation the law in Geneva had to be thoroughly overhauled. For example, Calvin was brought face to face with the need for a reformulation of the legal basis of courtship and marriage and with the consequent obligation to give advice in letters (along with Theodore Beza and Germain Colladon: all three were Frenchmen trained in the law), to be involved in legal judgments, and to show the biblical basis of his views in his sermons and commentaries, though less so in the *Institutes*.[27]

As part of this work Calvin was faced not only with enunciating principles but also with adjudicating on and advising on a multitude of hard 'cases'. What if a proposal of marriage was made frivolously, or when the proposal was made when drunk? Is it possible to promise marriage upon certain conditions? What of those wives who had become Protestant and were as a consequence abused by their husbands? Could they flee? (Calvin's answer was: only if a wife was in danger of her life should she leave her husband). If an engaged person was deserted by her fiancé, how long need she wait before seeking another husband? So Calvin's calling did not take him away from domestic joys or woes, and certainly not from domestic woes. (He had his own share of such hardships: none of his children survived infancy, and his own wife, Adelette de Bure, died young. His relations got into various scrapes.)

Calvin's general approach here has one further general implication of great significance. If it is lawful for us to go beyond the demands of strict necessity and to enjoy, with moderation, what the Lord in his goodness has provided, then it is lawful to provide those things for others. If the enjoyment of marble and ivory is legitimate, then it must be equally legitimate to be a merchant in ivory and a sculptor of marble. This argument has an important consequence: it makes possible the development of Calvin's (and Luther's, of course) idea of calling, or having a legitimate earthly vocation to which God has called a person. Not only the clergy have such a calling: the laity as well. Here is a Reformation insight with profound implications.

> Every man's mode of life, therefore, is a kind of station assigned him by the Lord, that he may not be always driven about at random. So necessary is this distinction, that all our actions are thereby estimated in his sight, and often in a very different way from which that in which human reason or philosophy would estimate them. . . . Again, in all our cares, toils, annoyances, and other burdens, it will be no small alleviation to know that all these are under the superintendence of God. The magistrate will more willingly perform his office, and the father of a family confine himself to his proper sphere. Every one in his particular mode of life will, without repining, suffer its inconveniences, cares, uneasiness, and anxiety, persuaded that God has laid on the burden. This, too, will afford admirable consolation, that in following your proper calling, no work will be so mean and sordid as not to have a splendour and value in the eye of God.[28]

No doubt there is a covert plea here for upholding the existing class and economic structures. Nevertheless, Calvin's positive view of daily callings was a great advance on the Roman distinction between the sacred and the secular, because it did not automatically regard any secular calling as inferior.

Although our discussion has been in terms of personal ethics, Calvin is sensitive to the social obligations to others and to the community. There is a strong social dimension to his thought, and a sense of compassion for the underdog that is strikingly at odds with popular impression of Calvin as dour and uncaring. In a course of sermons on the Gospels, which was uncompleted at the time he died, he says

> So when we see some who are sick or poor or destitute, and others who are in trouble and distress of body or mind, we should say, 'This person belongs to the same body as I do.' And then we should prove by our deeds that we are merciful. We can proclaim our pity for those who suffer time without number; but unless we actually assist them, our claims will be worthless. There are plenty of people who will say 'Oh dear! How terrible to be like that poor man!' Yet they simply brush it all aside, making no attempt to help. Expressions of pity stir none into action. In short, this world is full of mercy if words are to be believed; in reality it is all pretence.[29]

Such concern for the needy was given concrete expression in Geneva through, for example, the creation of the *Bourse français*, which was under the direction of the diaconate of the church and which cared for refugees and the poor of Geneva.[30]

PROVIDENCE, FATE AND THE LIFE TO COME

We noted when discussing predestination in Chapter 5 that in Calvin's thought it is strongly connected with his view of providence. It is an aspect of providence. God's providence over his creation is *particular* – 'meticulous', as it is sometimes called – reaching to every detail, and it is *secret*. In general, God does not disclose to us what he will do in advance, or why he will do it.

It follows that all the sorrows and evils that befall the Christian are, paradoxically perhaps, part of God's fatherly care of him. Providence is not simply divine government that conserves the creation, in all its detail, in existence, but it is also purposive. God in his sovereign mercy predestines his saints to glory, and his providential control of their lives is a means to that end. The bad things that happen to good people, then, are a part of God's heavenly wisdom, preparing them for their heavenly home. There is strong element of otherworldliness about Calvin's spirituality.

So the doctrine of providence is for Calvin not merely a matter of theoretical discussion, one locus in the theological text book, but it is meant to have operational value for the Christian. Someone who believes that nothing happens by chance, but that everything comes from the hand of God, will come to regard what befalls them differently from someone who thinks that evils may happen for no reason at all, or that how things turn out is a matter of luck, or that one's destiny is written in the stars, or that one makes one's own future. Yet Calvin brings out this value in sometimes surprising ways.

For example, one might think that his view of providence ought to lead to inactivity. If God has ordained all the details of my life, what is there for me to do? We might think that Calvin's attitude would be: If God is going to favour us, he is then going to favour us. If he is going to bring evil, then he is going to bring evil. Either way, there is nothing to be done. But this is not what he says. For instance, he thinks that we ought to have a very different attitude to the past than we have to the future.

> The Lord has furnished men with the arts of deliberation and caution, that they may employ them in subservience to his providence, in the preservation of their life; while, on the contrary, by neglect and sloth, they bring upon themselves the evils which he has annexed to them. How comes it that a provident man, while he consults for his safety, disentangles himself from impending evils; while a foolish man, through unadvised temerity, perishes, unless it be that prudence and folly are, in either case, instruments of divine dispensation? God has been pleased to conceal from us all future events that we may prepare for them as doubtful, and cease not to apply the provided remedies until they have either been overcome, or have proved too much for all our care.[31]

There is a general, divinely ordained, connection between means and ends, and we should respect this. But further than this, and very surprisingly, Calvin says that we ought to think about the future as if God's decree, his providential rule, does *not* extend to it!

> Wherefore, with reference to the time future, since the events of things are, as yet, hidden and unknown, everyone ought to be as intent upon the performance of his duty as if nothing whatever had been decreed concerning the issue in each particular case. Or (to speak more properly) every man ought so to hope for success in all things which he undertakes at the command of God, as to be

freely prepared to reconcile every contingency with the sure and certain Providence of God.[32]

Note here the references to duty and to the command of God. In the *Institutes* Calvin puts the point slightly differently.

I say then, that though all things are ordered by the counsel and certain arrangement of God, to us, however, they are fortuitous, – not because we imagine that Fortune rules the world and mankind, and turns all things upside down at random (far be such a heartless thought from every Christian breast); but as the order, method, end, and necessity of events, are, for the most part, hidden in the counsel of God, though it is certain that they are produced by the will of God, they have the appearance of being fortuitous, such being the form under which they present themselves to us, whether considered in their own nature, or estimated according to our knowledge and judgment.[33]

In order to make sense of what Calvin is claiming here, it is necessary to understand that he may use a phrase such as 'the will of God' to refer both to the *command* of God, that which sets out our duty, and to the *decree* of God, his plan, which is mostly hidden from us. If our future is hidden from us, how should we live? Calvin's answer is, by making the revealed will of God our guide, and by leaving the outcome to his wisdom and goodness.

Perhaps it is in relation to the evils of life that Calvin's view of providence (not a view which he invented, of course, but the regular doctrine of the Christian church which he took on) is most distinctive, as in this eloquent passage

We must use modesty, not as it were compelling God to render an account, but so revering his hidden judgments as to account his will the best of all reasons. When the sky is overcast with dense clouds, and a violent tempest arises, the darkness which is presented to our eye, and the thunder which strikes our ears, and stupifies all our senses with terror, make us imagine that everything is thrown into confusion, though in the firmament itself all continues quiet and serene. In the same way, when the tumultuous aspect of human affairs unfits us for judging, we should still hold that God, in the pure light of his justice and wisdom, keeps all these commotions in due subordination, and conducts them to their proper end.[34]

Besides encouraging moderation such a view of providence, properly internalised, will promote (Calvin says) humility, adoration, soberness, trust in God, gratitude for favourable outcomes, patience in adversity, 'incredible freedom from worry about the future,' submission to God, confidence in him, relief, freedom from anxiety, fearlessness, comfort and assurance.[35]

Calvin firmly held that our life here is to preparatory to our life hereafter, and one way in which he motivates his readers to virtue is by encouraging them to have regard for the life to come. He devotes a separate section to this in the *Institutes* in his account of the life of a Christian man. In a way which is largely foreign to modern Christian spirituality, Calvin believes that the ills of this life should prompt us to hope for the life to come, not of course to prompt us to project a life to come out of thin air, in the sense proposed by Feuerbach and Marx, but to intensify hope for what the Christian is convinced on good grounds is to come. 'Our mind never rises seriously to desire and aspire after the future, until it has learned to despise the present life.' This is part of 'the discipline of the cross'.[36] Because the present life has 'many allurements', our captivation to it must be broken. 'What, pray, would happen, if we here enjoyed an uninterrupted course of honour and felicity, when even the constant stimulus of affliction cannot arouse us to a due sense of our misery?'[37]

Calvin gives a wonderful, mordant depiction of what he regards as our tendency to self-deception about life. We attend a funeral and may then 'philosophise brilliantly' about the vanity of this life. But only for a moment.

> Forgetful not only of death, but also of mortality itself, as if no rumour of it had ever reached us, we indulge in supine security as expecting a terrestrial immortality. Meanwhile, if any one breaks in with the proverb, that man is the creature of a day, we indeed acknowledge its truth, but so far from giving heed to it, the thought of perpetuity still keeps hold of our minds.[38]

It is not that the idea of heaven arises from the need to project the life to come in order to cope with our unhappy lot. Rather that (in a thorough reversal of the modern attitude) we ought to come to a true estimate of the present life and be wrenched away from the fantasies that such a life will continue for ever. We must be 'shaken from our sluggishness', as he puts it.

Yet we should not hate our present life, or to flee from it, or to display ingratitude to God for it. 'This life, though abounding in all kinds of wretchedness, is justly classed among divine blessings which are not to be despised.' 'Nature herself exhorts us to return thanks to God for having brought us forth into light, granted us the use of it, and bestowed upon us all the means necessary for its preservation.'[39]

But

If heaven is our country, what can earth be but a place of exile? If departure from the world is entrance into life, what is the world but a sepulchre, and what is residence in it but immersion in death? If to be freed from the body is to gain full possession of freedom, what is the body but a prison? If it is the very summit of happiness to enjoy the presence of God, is it not miserable to want it?[40]

Again, no doubt with his own ill-health in mind,[41] he writes,

For if we reflect that this our tabernacle, unstable, defective, corruptible, fading, pining and putrid, is dissolved, in order that it may forthwith be renewed in sure, perfect, incorruptible, in fine, in heavenly glory, will not faith compel us eagerly to desire what nature dreads? . . . This, however, let us hold as fixed, that no man has made much progress in the school of Christ who does not look forward with joy to the day of death and final resurrection (2 Tim. 4.18; Tit. 2.13).[42]

The eloquence of these passages does not, however, disguise a tension in Calvin's thought at this point between the pull of the demands and joys of the present life, and the certain prospect of the greater joys of the life to come. We shall explore this tension next.

CHAPTER 7

THE CHURCH AND SOCIETY

According to Calvin's view of Christ's kingship, his rule extends over his kingdom, the church, and over wider society. I shall frame the discussion of Calvin's attitude to the relationship between the church and society in terms of two sets of tensions, institutional strains bequeathed by his theological claims. By a tension I mean a set of ideas, which while formally consistent will nevertheless ensure institutional instability, or make it likely. The first has to do with the relationship between Word and Spirit. The second arises from Calvin's view that the magistrate has the duty to uphold the moral law both in respect of duties to God and to duties to one's neighbour.

Happily, however, this chapter is not going to attempt to recount the history of actual tensions in Calvin's somewhat chequered personal history in Geneva, nor even the tortuous and tragic debates among the leaders of the Reformation about the Sacraments, though I believe that some of this history illustrates these tensions. We shall remain in the realm of John Calvin's ideas.

Finally, in the last section of the chapter, we shall broaden the connotation of 'society' to embrace not only the church and state and their relation, but also the world of culture and of learning, of business and the professions, and look at Calvin's attempt to relate the Christian and the Christian church to that world. Once again we shall note the possibility of serious tensions. So we shall be concerned with Calvin's doctrines, ideas that arose from his thinking and affected both his personal history and the history of 'Calvinism'.

What is to be discussed in this chapter was extremely important to Calvin. The Reformation as he understood it was not simply the re-formation of the doctrine of salvation along Scriptural lines, important though that was, but also the re-formation of the church and its relationship to society to reflect Reformation soteriology. It is no accident therefore that Book IV of the *Institutes*, from which nearly all of the data of this chapter will be drawn, occupies about a third of the length of the whole. One might even argue that Book IV is the culmination of the entire work.

THE CHURCH

We have already noted that the key to Calvin's understanding of the church is that it has a ministerial rather than a priestly character. The teachers and pastors of the church are ministers of the word of God, with a calling in parallel with other callings that Christians may have, to be dentists or draughtsmen, not a different class of Christian. They do not dispense salvation, for Christ alone, as the Head and King of the church, does this. But they minister his word and have authority only so far as they do so. They are to preach and teach in the hope and expectation that Christ's Spirit will by their means bring people to salvation, to union with Christ, and to membership of his body in its visible expression. So the church is vital, though vital in a different way than the Roman conception that Calvin heartily repudiates. It is consistent with this high view of the church that Calvin does not hesitate to refer to the church as the mother of the faithful

> into whose bosom God is pleased to collect his children, not only that by her aid and ministry they may be nourished so long as they are babes and children, but may also be guided by her maternal care until they grow up to manhood, and, finally, attain the perfection of faith. What God has thus joined, let not man put asunder (Mark 10.9): to those to whom he is a Father, the Church must also be a mother.[1]

So the church is not a loose association of individuals who meet for religious recreation but the visible expression of the body of Christ, whose 'marks' are the ministry of the apostolic word and the administration, at Christ's command, of the two sacraments of baptism and the Lord's Supper. The church is apostolic, proclaiming the faith of the prophets and apostles. For it is the material content of her ministry, not a pedigree that can be traced back to the apostles, that establishes the authenticity of the church, the communion of saints on earth.

Calvin sharply distinguishes this conception of the church from the assemblies of the Anabaptists as well as from the Church of Rome which (in his estimate) is not (in the main) a church because it does not manifest all the marks of the church. Though, as we have noted previously, Calvin is a man of high ideals, he is not a perfectionist, and he tempers this ideal of the church as one, holy, and catholic and apostolic, in important respects.

In the first place, though the church has within her those who are truly Christian, God's elect, membership of the visible church is not a guarantee of God's election. So Calvin operates with a distinction between the visible church, some of the features of which we have just been sketching, and the invisible church of God's elect, known to God only, embracing the people of God of all ages including those presently triumphant in heaven and those who, though Christian, may be presently unattached to the visible church. By contrast, the visible church comprises those who here and now make a credible profession of faith and who adhere to the society of the church.

It is possible to be one of God's elect and so to rely upon Christ, possessing the virtues of faith and love, and yet due to unusual circumstances not to be in communion with the visible church. Christians may be scattered because of persecution, as was the case, Calvin believed, with true believers in almost every country of Europe, and especially in his beloved France. They may be a Robinson Crusoe, marooned on an island. They may lack sufficient assurance to make a public profession of the faith. They may be believers in secret. Calvin himself, in his early life as a Christian, half in and half out of the Roman church, presumably fell into such an anomalous category. He notes the danger of being overscrupulous in the requirements for a public profession of Christianity,[2] and recognises the existence of delinquent churches.[3] So membership of the visible church of Christ, while it is usual, and required where possible, is neither necessary, nor sufficient, for membership of the invisible church, the company of God's elect.

I have observed that the Scriptures speak of the Church in two ways. Sometimes when they speak of the Church they mean the Church as it really is before God – the Church into which none are admitted but those who by the gift of adoption are sons of God, and by the sanctification of the Spirit true members of Christ. In this case it not only comprehends the saints who dwell on the earth, but all the elect who have existed from the beginning of the world. Often, too, by the name of Church is designated the whole body of mankind scattered throughout the world, who profess to worship one God and Christ, who by baptism are initiated into the faith; by partaking of the Lord's Supper profess unity in true doctrine and charity, agree in holding the word of the Lord, and observe the ministry which Christ has appointed for the preaching of it. In this Church there is a very large mixture of hypocrites, who have nothing of Christ but the name and outward appearance.[4]

Further, the Church of Rome is an apostate church, for 'the sum of necessary doctrine is inverted and the use of the sacraments is destroyed.'[5] Calvin distinguishes between that *church* and *churches.* Even though the Church of Rome, as an institution, is corrupt and to be repudiated, nevertheless he notes that 'in the present day we deny not to the Papists those vestiges of a Church which the Lord has allowed to remain among them amid the dissipation.'[6] The Lord

'preserved baptism there as an evidence of the covenant; – baptism, which, consecrated by his lips, retains its power in spite of human depravity; secondly, He provided by his providence that there should be other remains also to prevent the Church from utterly perishing'.[7] So 'while we are unwilling simply to concede the name of Church to the Papists, we do not deny that there are churches among them'.[8]

So the institutional church, while it has the marks of unity, catholicity and apostolicity, nevertheless has somewhat ragged boundaries and a complex make up. The visible church has within it God's elect, but is not comprised of all and only God's elect, some of whom may be members of no visible church. And while the Church of Rome is apostate, there are viable local churches within that 'church', churches that are nevertheless in communion with the See of Rome. Calvin tempers his theory of the church with a robust sense of the upheavals taking place all around him.

Given these ragged boundaries it is difficult to claim that Calvin has a clearly defined sense of what constitutes being 'in' or 'out of' the institutional church. And although there is little or no evidence for the idea that Calvin thought there was a set of people, 'anonymous

Christians', who though they do not avow the Christian faith are nevertheless to be regarded as Christians themselves, to those with a more watertight view of the boundaries of the society of the church it may nevertheless seem that he leaves open this possibility.

THE TWO SACRAMENTS

Discord over the sacraments, chiefly over the Lord's Supper, less so over baptism, at least among the magisterial reformers, contributed to these ecclesiastical upheavals. Before we look at the factors that resulted in that discord, we must try to gain a general picture of Calvin's approach to the sacraments. A sacrament is, he says, 'an external sign, by which the Lord seals on our consciences his promises of good-will towards us, in order to sustain the weakness of our faith, and we in our turn testify our piety toward him, both before himself, and before angels as well as men.'[9]

The sacramental ceremonies are in no sense magical, and not *ex opere operato*. They are means of grace, they minister grace to those who truly partake of them, and their sacramental efficacy does not derive from priestly consecration, nor from the personal spirituality of the minister, but from the word of God and from the state of the recipient. These means are thus subordinate to the word of God as this is read, preached, understood and received by the congregation. Consistently with this, the magisterial reformers allow that baptism, and even the Lord's Supper, may be validly celebrated by ministers who are personally unfitted, either morally or theologically, to provide ministerial leadership in the church.

You see how he [viz. Augustine] requires preaching to the production of faith. And we need not labour to prove this, since there is not the least room for doubt as to what Christ did, and commanded us to do, as to what the apostles followed, and a purer Church observed. Nay, it is known that, from the very beginning of the world, whenever God offered any sign to the holy Patriarchs, it was inseparably attached to doctrine, without which our senses would gaze bewildered on an unmeaning object. Therefore, when we hear mention made of the sacramental word, let us understand the promise which, proclaimed aloud by the minister, leads the people by the hand to that to which the sign tends and directs us.[10]

In common with all the Reformers Calvin rejects the Roman doctrine of transubstantiation. He offers numerous objections to it; that it was unknown in Christian antiquity, that it has no Scriptural basis, and that its metaphysics is unintelligible.[11] But his chief objection is Christological, that it compromises the true humanity, the true embodiment in human flesh, of the incarnate Word.

But assuming that the body and blood of Christ are attached to the bread and wine, then the one must necessarily be dissevered from the other. For as the bread is given separately from the cup, so the body, united to the bread, must be separated from the blood, included in the cup. For since they affirm that the body is in the bread, and the blood is in the cup, while the bread and wine are, in regard to space, at some distance from each other, they cannot, by any quibble, evade the conclusion that the body must be separated from the blood.[12]

Nevertheless, although Calvin insists that Christ's body is one physical organism, and spatially bounded, yet by his Ascension and Session at the Father's right hand Christ has taken possession of a Kingdom that is

not limited by any intervals of space, nor circumscribed by any dimensions. Christ can exert his energy wherever he pleases, in earth and heaven, can manifest his presence by the exercise of his power, can always be present with his people, breathing into them his own life, can live in them, sustain, confirm and invigorate them, and preserve them safe, just as if he were with them in the body.[13]

So Christ, while embodied, nevertheless 'reigns in the Father's power and majesty and glory', and exerts his influence by his Spirit at every point of his earthly Kingdom. In particular, as regards the sacraments, the Spirit presents the real presence of the 'whole Christ' to faithful participants of the Supper even while Christ himself is physically absent.

Calvin's view of the Supper may be placed somewhere between the consubstantiation of the Lutherans, according to which the body of the glorified Christ, taking on the divine property of immensity, is present together with the bread of the Supper, and the 'memorialism' of the Zwnglians. Calvin kept up a running battle with two Lutherans, Joachim Westphal (1510–74) and Tileman Heshusius (1527–88). He abhorred memorialism to such a great degree that he refused for a while to read any of the Zwinglian writings. The divisions among the various Reformers and their respective parties were tragic for the coherence of the Reformation movement, but it is possible to understand why it was that Calvin differed over what for him were points of principle that could not easily be patched up with face-saving forms of words.

The Lutherans held that the incarnate Christ was physically present *with* and *under* the bread and the wine once they are consecrated, but not that the substance of the elements is changed into the very flesh and blood of the Saviour, hence '*con*substantiation' rather than '*tran*substantiation'. Their view entailed the ubiquity of the risen Christ, especially the ubiquity of his body. Christ is seated at the right hand of the Father in heaven and as a result his glorified body is also able to be physically present wherever the Lord's Supper is celebrated.

The theory behind this lay in a particular understanding of the ancient doctrine of the communication of attributes, the *communicatio idiomatum*. As we noted in Chapter 4, Calvin held that because Christ is *autotheos*, God himself, in virtue of his union with human nature in one person, and as a kind of testimony to it, Scripture occasionally ascribes human properties to the divine, and (less commonly) divine properties of the human. So Paul speaks of the Church of God that he has purchased with his own blood, as if God has blood. (Acts 20.28) We saw that Calvin treated these expressions as vivid, rhetorical language, but the Lutherans made a metaphysical theory out of them according to which through Christ's glorification his human nature gains divine attributes or properties, particularly ubiquity. This Calvin vehemently denied.

> But because fixing the body itself in the bread, they attach to it an ubiquity contrary to its nature, and by adding *under* the bread, will have it that it lies hid under it. . . . They insist, then, that the body of Christ is invisible and immense, so that it may be hid under bread, . . . Because they cannot conceive any other participation of flesh and blood than that which consists either in local conjunction and contact, or in some gross method of enclosing.[14]

But, Calvin maintained, Christ's body, a normal human body, though glorified, was circumscribed as necessarily all human bodies are.[15] The Lutherans misunderstand the idea of the communication of properties.

> But some are so hurried away by contention as to say, that on account of the union of the natures in Christ, wherever his divinity is, there his flesh, which cannot be separated from it, is also; as if that union formed a kind of medium of the two natures, making him to be neither God nor man. . . . In regard to the passages which they adduce . . . they betray the same stupidity, scouting the communion of properties (*idiomatum*), which not without reason was formerly invented by the holy Fathers. Certainly when Paul says of the princes of this world that they 'crucified the Lord of glory' (I Cor. 2.8), he means not that he suffered anything, in his divinity, but that Christ, who was rejected and despised, and suffered in the flesh, was likewise God and the Lord of glory.[16]

There are two features of Calvin's Christology evident here, each of which we have met before. The first is his clear sense, derived from Scripture and expressed in Chalcedonian conceptuality, that the divine person and the human nature of Christ, though united in the one person of the Mediator, are unchangeably distinct. Christ, having a human nature, is unchangeably human and so unchangeably localised. Second, Calvin emphasises, as the Church Fathers did before him, that Christ's divinity, being true divinity, was infinite and immense even when incarnate. Consequently, although the Mediator is fully divine, the Incarnation did not enclose that divinity, confining it within the bounds of Christ's physical body. This point the Lutherans dubbed the *extra calvinisticum* , the Calvinistic addition.

Calvin makes use of a scholastic distinction to try to cast light on it, a distinction that he repeatedly uses in his controversy with Westphal.

> There is a trite distinction in the schools which I hesitate not to quote. Although the whole Christ is everywhere, yet everything which is in him, is not everywhere. . . . Therefore, while our whole Mediator is everywhere, he is always present with his people, and in the Supper exhibits his presence in a special manner; yet so, that while he is wholly present, not everything which is in him is

present, because, as has been said, in his flesh he will remain in heaven till he come to judgment.[17]

Commenting on Ephesians 4.10 he writes,

When we hear of the ascension of Christ, it instantly strikes our minds that he is removed to a great distance from us; and so he actually is, with respect to his body and human presence. But Paul reminds us, that, while he is removed from us in bodily presence, he *fills all things* by the power of his Spirit. Wherever the right hand of God, which embraces heaven and earth, is displayed, Christ is spiritually present by his boundless power; although, as respects his body, the saying of Peter holds true, that 'the heaven must receive him until the times of restitution of all things, which God hath spoken by the mouth of all his holy prophets since the world began'.(Acts 3.21)[18]

So how is the whole Christ present? The whole Christ is present, but not in his wholeness! How can this be? Calvin's answer remains a matter of scholarly debate, but I think that the key to his position lies in another central feature of his Christology, or at least to his distinctive stress on that feature. We noted in Chapter 5 that at the heart of Calvin's understanding of the Christian life is a stress on the individual's union with Christ. From that union, bequeathed to him by the Father's decree, and made actual by the Spirit's presence, come the two distinct but inseparable graces of justification and sanctification. Calvin understands the distinct significance of the Supper to be related to this union.

Expounding the nature of this 'spiritual banquet', a 'high mystery', Calvin writes,

But as this mystery of the secret union of Christ with believers is incomprehensible by nature, he exhibits its figure and image in visible signs adapted to our capacity, nay, by giving, as it were, earnests and badges, he makes it as certain to us as if it were seen by the eye; the familiarity of the similitude giving it access to minds however dull, and showing that souls are fed by Christ just as the corporeal life is sustained by bread and wine. We now, there-fore, understand the end which this mystical benediction has in view – viz. to assure us that the body of Christ was once sacrificed for us, so that we may now eat it, and, eating, feel within ourselves the efficacy of that one sacrifice, – that his blood was once shed for us so as to be our perpetual drink.[19]

Union with Christ is the key, and the Supper exhibits and supports that union, and its true efficacy is made possible by it. 'Pious souls can derive great confidence and delight from this sacrament, as being a testimony that they form one body with Chirst, so that everything which is in him they may call their own.'[20]

What then, of the presence of Christ, if *contra* the Lutherans, his body is localised in heaven? Calvin's answer is: Christ is nevertheless really present through the power of his Spirit.

But though it seems an incredible thing that the flesh of Christ, while at such a distance from us in respect of place, should be food to us, let us remember how far the secret virtue of the Holy Spirit surpasses all our conceptions, and how foolish it is to wish to measure its immensity by our feeble capacity. Therefore, what our mind does not comprehend let faith conceive – viz. that the Spirit truly unites things separated by space.[21]

The Holy Spirit presents to believers' minds the efficacy of Christ's work who, though localised in his body in heaven, is present to them by his Spirit, and so 'really' present. The presence does not consist in subjective changes in the believer's psyche, nor in physical presence, but in a Spirit-induced union with Christ. The Lord's Supper is not magical, but it is most certainly mysterious: 'incomprehensible' in Calvin's technical understanding of that term: something that though we may have some apprehension of, we cannot get our minds around, but which nonetheless leads him to expressions of the deepest feeling.

Nay, I rather exhort my readers not to confine their apprehension within those too narrow limits, but to attempt to rise much higher than I can guide them. For whenever this subject is considered, after I have done my utmost, I feel that I have spoken far beneath its dignity. And though the mind is more powerful in thought than the tongue in expression, it too is overcome and overwhelmed by the magnitude of the subject. All then that remains is to break forth in admiration of the mystery, which it is plain that the mind is inadequate to comprehend, or the tongue to express.[22]

What of Baptism? Were we to confine our attention to what Calvin writes in *Institutes* IV.15 on baptism, we would be left with the impression that he holds exclusively to believer's baptism, though he was most certainly not an Anabaptist. The entire discussion is framed in terms of the believer: 'Those who receive baptism with true faith truly feel the efficacy of Christ's death in the mortification of their flesh, and the efficacy of his resurrection in the quickening of the Spirit.'[23] It is a token of our union with Christ.[24]

> Believers become assured by baptism, that this condemnation is entirely withdrawn from them, since (as has been said) the Lord by this sign promises that a full and entire remission has been made, both of the guilt which was imputed to us, and the penalty incurred by the guilt.[25]

Baptism is our confession before men, it is to be received with trust. Calvin leaves until the next chapter, IV.16, which he calls an 'appendix',[26] his understanding and defence of infant baptism.

Though believer's baptism may be the paradigm, the baptism of infants is legitimised by Scripture and is warranted. The children of believers are 'holy' (I Cor.7.14) and they are the heirs of God's promise.

> The salvation of infants is included in the promise in which God declares to believers that he will be a God to them and to their seed. In this way he declared, that those deriving descent from Abraham were born to him. (Gen. 17.7) In virtue of this promise they are admitted to baptism, because they are considered members of the Church. Their salvation, therefore, has not its commencement in baptism, but being already founded on the word, is sealed by baptism.[27]

Nevertheless, here is an area of potential tension, between an individualistic understanding of the sacrament of baptism and an understanding in terms of family unity and parental responsibility and sponsorship.

Finally, there is the question of church discipline, the keys. Discipline is essential to the *bene esse* of the church, not to its *esse*, as is made clear in his debates with the Anabaptists regarding their use of the 'ban'. Discipline has various stages: private admonition, public admonition, and ultimately, if a person persists in his iniquity, he is then, as a despiser of the Church, to be debarred from the society of believers.[28] Calvin is clear, once again, that such power is ministerial. It is bound up with the proclamation of the Word, and 'we must always beware of dreaming of any power apart from the preaching of the Gospel.'[29] The purpose of discipline is corrective and restorative, not retributive.[30] But if a person is obdurate, then excommunication must follow. In the close-knit community of Geneva, with the frequent celebration of the Lord's Supper which Calvin favoured, excommunication would be a highly visible action with immediate and severe social consequences, whether or not these consequences were, strictly speaking, intended as a part of the process of excommunication.

Throughout Calvin's discussion of the church, one motif recurs: Word and Spirit. The church is where the Word is preached and where through the Word, and the Spirit's illumination and application of it, people are regenerated and as a result experience life-long *conversio*.

We have noted a tension in Calvin's understanding of, or at least in his presentation of, baptism. However, here, in this broader emphasis on Word and Spirit is a source of a more serious tension, of potential breakdown which as far as I am aware Calvin does not recognise and certainly does not address.

In the central motif of 'Word and Spirit' the two elements can only be linked together rather uneasily. The reason is this: matters to do with 'the Word' can be humanly organised. But matters to do with 'the Spirit' are divinely sovereign and free, out of human hands. Of course, there is a sense in which, through Calvin's general view of God's sovereignty and his idea of providence, everything is decreed by God. So perhaps we should put the point more exactly. Matters to do with the Word may be dispensed through secondary, creaturely agency alone, but matters to do with the Spirit can never be so dispensed. The idea that they could be is, for Calvin, the root failure of the sacramentalism of the Papacy. People can be trained for the Christian ministry, study the Bible and preach it. Churches can be set up; pastors, teachers and deacons appointed; the sacraments may be administered; people catechised and the unruly disciplined. All this can be undertaken in a routine, institutional way and carried out with the positive support of the magistrate. All very orderly, in the Calvinian manner. All these are, we might say, the area of 'the Word'.

But what of 'the Spirit'? Here there is a dramatic difference. For God the Spirit, though he attends the Word, is free not to do so. Nowhere, as far as I know, does Calvin teach that the linkage between Word and Spirit is automatic or necessary, or that God is under an obligation always to accompany the Word with the salvific influence of the Spirit. God has covenanted to accompany his Word by His Spirit, but the exact distribution of the Spirit's saving influence is still at his disposal.

But who, I ask, can deny the right of God to have the free and uncontrolled disposal of his gifts, to select the nations which he may be pleased to illuminate, the places which he may be pleased to illustrate by the preaching of his word, and the mode and measure of progress and success which he may be pleased to give to his doctrine, – to punish the world for its ingratitude, by withdrawing the knowledge of his name for certain ages, and again, when he so pleases, to restore it in mercy?[31]

And in the case of the authority of Holy Scripture, while it is possible for human agencies to educate people in an appreciation of the external proofs, it is not possible in a similar way for them to convey the internal testimony of the Holy Spirit. That testimony cannot be, so to speak, boxed and wrapped.

Similarly with Calvin's depiction of the entire life of a Christian. Men and women can be brought to observe the law, particularly if the church has the backing of the magistrate, but neither the minister nor the magistrate can impart a godly motivation. It is possible to administer the sacraments as institutional rites of the church, but their efficacy, by Calvin's own reckoning, depends upon penitence, faith, union with Christ and the mortification and vivification of the believer. Areas of serious tension, then.

THE MAGISTRATE

Calvin presents his view of the magistrate in the last chapter of the *Institutes*. This short section is by no means a full-blown treatise on political theory, nor even the sketch of one. For example, Calvin does not deal with how the state arises, whether it is a consequence of fallenness or not. Nonetheless, Calvin takes the magistracy with extreme seriousness and is keen to separate himself from anything that smacks of Anabaptism.

In general, Calvin's idea is that the church should not dominate the state in the Papal manner, nor the state dominate the church in the Erastian manner. Instead there should be a formal separation of them in terms of function, but also an alliance, or at least a recognised coincidence of interest, between the magistrate and the church. They are to be distinct but linked. What is to hold them in tandem is their recognition of the authority of the divine moral law, in both its tables.

As we have seen this law is to be administered by the church in her exercise of discipline. It is also to be administered through a set of social and legal norms enacted by the magistrate, with punishments, including capital punishment, being affixed to transgressions. The magistrate has the power to make and administer both tables of the law,[32] to levy taxes,[33] and to wage war, albeit in a humane and just manner.[34]

Calvin is clear that the role of the magistrate is only properly carried out when he includes in his duties the upholding of true religion. The magistrate is not an officer of the church, but he is nevertheless a 'minister of God' in a rather different sense, an agent of God one of whose duties is to uphold the true worship of God. Furthermore, the magistrate 'if he is pious'[35] will himself be a member of the church and so subject to its discipline.

How does Calvin argue that the magistrate should have a concern for both tables of the Law, duties to God as well as duties to man? There seem to be two sets of arguments. First, arguments from precedent. 'Among philosophers religion holds the first place, and that the same thing has always been observed with the universal consent of nations, Christian princes and magistrates may be ashamed of their heartlessness if they make it not their care'.[36] Calvin probably has Cicero's *Laws* in view here. In addition, there is the precedent of the 'holy kings' of the Old Testament, the Israelite theocracy.

The arguments from precedent don't seem very strong, since Cicero is hardly an infallible guide, and perhaps the precedents are bad precedents. Further, the kings of the Old Testament are part of a theocracy, and (though Calvin's Geneva is routinely referred to by commentators as a theocracy), Calvin expressly denies that the magistrate governs theocratically.[37] He stresses the legitimacy of different forms of government[38] and of different kinds of punishment.[39] As for Romans 14, Paul's teaching that the powers that be are ordained by God is by itself surely not sufficient. To accept that political power is ordained by God does not entail that such power ought to extend the enforcement of both Tables of the law.

Calvin has another argument, however. Behind the diversity of laws, and the diversity of forms of legitimate government to be found throughout the nations, lies the Decalogue itself. It is the rule of equity, 'the true and eternal rule of righteousness prescribed to the men of all nations and of all times, who would frame their life agreeably to the will of God. For his eternal and immutable will is, that we are all to worship him, and mutually love one another.'[40] All laws are therefore to be judged by the rule of equity as expressed in both tables of the Decalogue. Further,

> Now, as it is evident that the law of God which we call the moral, is nothing else than the testimony of natural law, and of that conscience which God has engraven on the minds of men, the whole of this equity of which we now speak is prescribed in it. Hence it alone ought to be the aim, the rule, and the end of all laws.[41]

So Calvin's argument is that the Moral Law is simply the natural law which is the rule of equity. As it is natural (though in fact it has also been revealed) it is capable of being recognised by everyone, by both magistrates and people, as the basis of good legislation.

All too obviously this is another area of potential tension and conflict, of actual conflict if one recalls the history of Calvin's dealings with the city authorities of Geneva. Among the sources of this tension is a situation in which membership of the Reformed church is virtually coterminous with citizenship. As we have noted, excommunication, even though Calvin regards it only as a churchly act, has clear social and political consequences. Calvin explicitly endorsed Augustine's interpretation of Christ's words 'compel them to come in', seeing it as a warrant for the magistrate to enforce church attendance legally.[42]

Further, in theory and often in practice, the same offence may call both for the censure of the church, even for excommunication, and for punishment at the hands of the magistrate. Yet the two actions, excommunication and judicial punishment, are distinct. One can readily see problems arising from the idea that the magistrate's function is to uphold (and in that sense be a minister of) orthodox Christian religion.

So there are several places of serious tension in this area of Calvin's thought and practice. Yet these ought not to be exaggerated. For the last of these, at least, the problems of state and church, are similar to the perennial problems generated in modern secular democratic states between authority and freedom. And keeping religion in view, they are similar in form to those currently familiar problem areas between the theoretically politically 'privatised' religions of the liberal democratic state and the political claims that these religions may make. For Calvin, the pressures arise from having a strong view of the duties of the magistrate. In the modern world, they arise from a secular view of the state's authority and the existence of religious pluralism, together with the insistence of many that religion is not merely private but has implications for the public square. But the sources of tension, between the scope of the state and the claims of religion, are the same.

THE CASE OF MICHAEL SERVETUS

Grasping Calvin's understanding of the responsibilities of the state to uphold true religion enables us to understand, if not to exonerate, his part in the dreadful Servetus affair. Michael Servetus was a Spaniard, perhaps also a Jew. Though he denied this, he was learned in rabbinic sources and argued that Christianity ought to be rooted in Judaism, though not in the pagan thought that led to the sophistry of the Council of Nicaea. He harried Roman Catholic and Protestant leaders alike with his unorthodox views. For a time he went under the pseudonym of Michel de Villeneuve. A sharp-minded and widely read person, interested in medicine and astrology, and evidently something of a know-all, he went from place to place promoting his heterodoxies – Basel, Strasbourg, Paris, Lyon, Montpellier and finally to Vienne. He provoked church leaders and others by his writings, especially the *Restoration of Christianity* (1553), with his anti-trinitarianism and his Arianism. In correspondence with Calvin, he returned his gift of the *Institutes* with the margins filled with his critical scribblings.

Perhaps the reason that Servetus was so severely treated was to show that, when it came to denying the Trinity and the full deity of Christ, Geneva could act every bit as decisively as the Roman Church. There is some evidence for this from the correspondence between

Guillaume de Trie, a friend of Calvin's, and his Roman Catholic cousin Antoine Arneys of Lyon. Antoine had reproached Guillaume for the fact that Geneva had no church discipline. Guillaume replied that though Servetus was tolerated in Roman Catholic territories he deserved to be burned.[43] Later, in March 1553, de Trie provided evidence (which he wrested from a reluctant Calvin) to the Roman authorities who were attempting to arraign Servetus. Servetus escaped from his trial and was arrested while passing through Geneva in August. Knowing Calvin's views as he did, it seems incredible that Servetus should turn up in Geneva. Perhaps he thought he could gain refuge in this bastion of anti-Romanism. If so, it was a fatal mistake.

To us it seems unthinkable that someone should be burnt at the stake for unorthodoxy, even though we are familiar with gulags, gas-chambers and other forms of mass extermination. The sixteenth century was the age of such burnings, and of the rack and the thumb-screw of the Inquisition. The singling out of the Servetus affair can only be put down to the fact that it was Calvin who was involved. He wrote to Farel in February 1546, (and this is hard to stomach as well),

> Servetus lately wrote to me, and coupled with his letter a long volume of delirious fancies, with the Thrasonic boast, that I should see something astonishing and unheard of. He takes it upon him to come hither, if it be agreeable to me. But I am unwilling to pledge my word for his safety, for if he shall come, I shall never permit him to depart alive, provided my authority be of any avail.[44]

It is important to understand that both his trial in Geneva and the sentence were acts of the magistrate, not the church. Servetus was not a member of the church in Geneva. On the other hand, nor was he a spy or a religious subversive as the Jesuits were in Elizabethan England. He does not seem to have provoked riots or other kinds of civil disorder. He was not the equivalent of a modern terrorist. It is not even clear whether or not his views gained any following in Geneva or elsewhere.

The plain fact is that the civil authorities in Geneva, with the support of Calvin, (though there looks to have been some friction between the two at this time), held that it was part of their duty to uphold both Tables of the Law. It was clear to them that his trial showed that Servetus was guilty of breaking that law. Calvin is hardly vindicated by his plea (which fell on deaf ears) that the offender ought not to burn but to be executed. Servetus' death is the chillingly consistent outcome of the doctrine of religious intolerance coupled with a readiness to impose capital punishment.

We have stressed in a number of places the danger of anachronism in forming an estimate of Calvin and his influence. It is a danger here as well. Judged by later standards of greater toleration the Servetus affair is monstrous. From this later standpoint, condemning Calvin is an easy shot. It might be said that the puzzle was not that the authorities acted consistently, but that they held, with Calvin's complete support, the views they did in the first place. But in this also they were children of their time. Yet to understand Calvin in the setting of his times is not to excuse him. He is convicted when measured against his own standards. He who held that the natural knowledge of God makes us all inexcusable was surely inexcusable himself in upholding the capital punishment of Servetus in the face of the revealed knowledge of God in Jesus Christ.

But times changed. In 1678 the sceptically minded Calvinist Pierre Bayle was able to write,

> The Punishment of *Servetus*, and of a very small number besides of the same stamp, erring in the most fundamental Points of the Christian Religion, is look'd on at this day as a horrid Blot upon the earlier days of the Reformation, the sad and deplorable Remains of Popery.[45]

TYRANNY AND RESISTANCE

It is an odd feature of the 1559 *Institutes* that Calvin continues to address this last edition of his work to King Francis I of France in fulsome terms similar to those he had used in the first edition of 1536: 'The Most Mighty and Illustrious Monarch, Francis, King of the French, His Sovereign; John Calvin Prays Peace and Salvation in Christ.' But among the words of the last chapter of the 1559 edition are, 'Let princes hear and be afraid.'[46]

Calvin holds that there must be obedience even to an unjust magistrate.[47] Are there limits to this? What is Calvin's view of tyranny?

> I speak only of private men. For when popular magistrates have been appointed to curb the tyranny of kings (as the Ephori, who

were opposed to kings among the Spartans, or Tribunes of the people to consuls among the Romans, or Demarchs to the senate among the Athenians; and perhaps there is something similar to this in the power exercised in each kingdom by the three orders, when they hold their primary diets). So far am I from forbidding these officially to check the undue license of kings, that if they connive at kings when they tyrannise and insult over the humbler of the people, I affirm that their dissimulation is not free from nefarious perfidy, because they fraudulently betray the liberty of the people, while knowing that, by the ordinance of God, they are its appointed guardians.[48]

Note the reference here to private individuals. Calvin is against *popular* uprisings, no doubt having Munster and the Peasants' War in mind. For Calvin society was stratified into the common people and the aristocracy from which the magistrate, the legislature and the executive were drawn. It was unthinkable for him that the daughter of a grocer should become Prime Minister, or that someone might be translated from a log cabin to the White House. What he objects to is popular rebellion, not constitutionally founded resistance to tyranny. It is such resistance that tyrannical kings ought to fear. But it has to be said that he does not fill out this position with concrete advice or constitutional detail.

However, to complete the picture of Calvin's overall outlook, we should bear in mind what we have learned about 'Nicodemism'. His conviction that Reformed Christians ought to be absent from the Mass rather than compromise their faith is politically significant. Public, passive resistance, if endured by enough people, may become politically potent. Calvin seems to have been prepared to countenance popular non-resistance if not popular rebellion.

To conclude this chapter, we move into rather happier territory.

THE TWO KINGDOMS

We return to the relation between 'things below' and 'things above,' briefly discussed at the end of Chapter 6. 'For there exists in man a kind of two worlds, over which different kings and different laws can preside.'[49] This sentence is at first sight extraordinary. Is Calvin saying that King Jesus only rules the church, while Francis I rules (say) over the kingdom of France? Maybe so, but certainly all events are ordained and governed by God, and (as we shall see) the Holy Spirit directly influences 'things below'. Further, the authority of the state is one aspect of Calvin's doctrine of the two kingdoms, of Christ's kingly rule, and that rule legitimises some kinds of political and other activity within society and disqualifies other kinds. The Christian must neither withdraw from society nor seek to form a separate, pure, churchly sect, as the Anabaptists do.

Towards the end of Chapter 6 we met with another way of thinking of the Christian and society, one which overlaps with this, the idea of the legitimacy of the Christian's secular calling as he concerns himself with 'things below'. Surely Calvin cannot deny that Jesus rules here too? Yet in a more central way Jesus exercises his kingly authority through the church, and through the regenerating and sanctifying influence of the Spirit on the members of the Body of Christ his Spirit prepares men and women for a heavenly kingdom. Unlike Augustine's two cities, which are antithetical, Calvin's two kingdoms overlap. The Christian finds himself occupying a place in each of them. How is he to manage this dual membership?

This is the shape of Calvin's answer to that question. There is

> one kind of intelligence of earthly things, and another of heavenly things. By earthly things, I mean those which relate not to God and his kingdom, to true righteousness and future blessedness, but have some connected with the present life, and are in a manner confined within its boundaries. By heavenly things, I mean the pure knowledge of God, the method of true righteousness, and the mysteries of the heavenly kingdom. To the former belong matters of policy and economy, all mechanical arts and liberal studies. To the latter belong the knowledge of God and of his will, and the means of framing the life in accordance with them.[50]

The idea of the distinction between earthly and heavenly kingdoms is very similar to Luther's.

> These two kingdoms must be sharply distinguished, and both be permitted to remain; the one to produce piety, the other to bring about external peace and prevent evil deeds; neither is sufficient in the world without the other. For no one can become pious before God by means of the secular government, without Christ's spiritual rule. Hence Christ's rule does not extend over all, but Christians are always in the minority and are in the midst of non-Christians.[51]

Perhaps Calvin has a more optimistic view of some of the products of the earthly kingdom than the German Reformer. To start with, the moral law does not simply restrain sin in society, but it enhances social life. In addition, he holds that besides the general effects of divine restraint and goodness there are 'special effects'. Particular individuals are gifted with special insight, or artistic or other creative skills, or with gifts of leadership and sagacity. These gifts are not generally dispersed but given selectively and sovereignly by God's goodness.

That Calvin may have these two sorts of thing in mind by his term 'general grace' is borne out, for example, by his remarks on Genesis 4.20 which states that Jabal, a son of Cain, is the father of such as dwell in tents.

Let us then know, that the sons of Cain, though deprived of the Spirit of regeneration, were yet endued with gifts of no despicable kind; just as the experience of all ages teaches us how widely the rays of divine light have shone on unbelieving nations, for the benefit of the present life; and we see, at the present time, that the excellent gifts of the Spirit are diffused through the whole human race. Moreover liberal arts and sciences have descended to us from the heathen. We are, indeed, compelled to acknowledge that we have received astronomy, and the other parts of philosophy, medicine, and the order of civil government, from them.[52]

Calvin has a variety of ways of expressing the fact of 'common grace': the restraint of evil, the positive influence of the moral law in society, and the gifting in unusual or exceptional ways of individual men and women in the sciences and fine arts, in government and in philosophy. As one might expect from him, the common factor in all this is a theological point. It is that all these gifts, which in themselves fall short of or are certainly different from the gift of the Spirit's regeneration and are no guarantee of it, are nevertheless gifts which are properly to be attributed to the Spirit of God.

Calvin has a generous, if somewhat puritanical, attitude to 'things below'. He is by no means a pietist or a fundamentalist. The 'world' is not an area to retreat from but to engage with, with a true motive, within the bounds of the moral law. The Christian must utilise the gifts and graces that God has provided to each one of us, engaging with all aspects of his creation and providential rule, enjoying his gifts as well as using them. There is no ethical dualism in Calvin, no Manicheism, no deeply rooted opposition between the material and the spiritual. For the one universe, matter and spirit, is God's creation. Though it is fallen, God's creation is to be enjoyed and used in the ways we have explored.

But this is not the whole story, nor is it the chief story. For there is no doubt that, as his terminology indicates, for Calvin there is a qualitative difference between the 'things above' and the 'things below'. 'If heaven is our country, what can the earth be but a place of exile? If departure from the world is entrance into life, what is the world but a sepulchre, and what is residence in it but immersion in death?'[53]

So we might wonder whether even if there is no Manichean dualism here, a dualism of another kind remains, that between the transient and the permanent. This world is passing, the world to come will abide. Is it also Calvin's view that all and only what directly promotes a concern for the world to come is of true value? Does he have any thought that some cultural products, the results of the operations of common grace, 'carry through' into the life to come, to form part of the environment of that life? Bach and Brahms and Dante and Milton? Gerry Mulligan and Pink Floyd? Is such a suggestion too fanciful to be authentically Calvinian?

It is hard to say. Calvin's eschatology is notoriously thin. But there are a couple of places – perhaps there are more – in which he certainly thinks of the renewed creation as carrying through to the world to come.

Shall the lower animals, and inanimate creatures themselves, even wood and stone, as conscious of their present vanity, long for the final resurrection, that they may with the sons of God be delivered from vanity (Rom. 8.19); and shall we, endued with the light of intellect, and more than intellect, enlightened by the Spirit of God, when our essence is in question, rise no higher than the corruption of this earth?[54]

Is it too fanciful to suppose that Calvin would be receptive to a parallel 'releasing from emptiness' of some of the artefacts of human culture, the products of the Holy Spirit of beauty and truth?

CHAPTER 8

CALVIN AND CALVINISM

Calvin died on 27 May 1564, aged 54. He was undernourished and had been very ill with tuberculosis, aggravated by other factors, by gout and fevers and colic. Above all, he was worn out through the strain of continuous preaching. Early in 1564 he was preaching on I Kings, on Ezekiel and on the Gospel harmony. He had to be carried around from one place of duty to another and then as his health further worsened he became bed-ridden.

On 27 April he was visited by Geneva's Little Council. He thanked them for their many kindnesses. He confessed his devotion to God and to Geneva, sought pardon for his various weaknesses and attempted to vindicate his part in the Reformation of the city.

> As to my doctrine, I have taught faithfully, and God has given me grace to write what I have written as faithfully as it was in my power. I have not falsified a single passage of the Scriptures, nor given it a wrong interpretation to the best of my knowledge; and though I might have introduced subtle senses, had I studied subtlety, I cast that temptation under my feet and always aimed at simplicity.[1]

His body lay in state only for a day or so before being buried in an unmarked grave in Plainpalais, the public cemetery, 'where he lies now, awaiting the resurrection he taught us about and so constantly hoped for'.[2]

CALVIN AND GENEVA

In the course of twenty years or so John Calvin had emerged from a life of scholarly retirement, as someone who endeavoured to promote the Reformation from the back room, to take centre stage in Geneva. That city became an international hub for the dissemination of Reformation teaching. Timid and fearful, yet resolute; excitable and bad-tempered, yet reticent about his own feelings; frugal and disciplined, Calvin continued to work incredibly hard, and with great speed, right to the end. His instinct was conservative and somewhat aristocratic, not to say autocratic. We know a great deal about his time in Geneva, his theological output and his work in implementing his vision of the Reformation in that city. But because of his reticence about himself, we know little of his own personal reflections. He wrote no *Confessions*, there is no *Table Talk*, though a considerable correspondence has been preserved for us.

At the heart of his influence was a ceaseless flow of writing – brief, clear, commentaries, fierce (and sometimes funny) polemical works, printed expository sermons – advice sought and given by letter, and especially the numerous editions and translations and abbreviations of his *Institutes*. Calvin's conception of Christianity 'reformed by the Word of God' came to prevail over those of other centres such as Basle, Strasbourg and Zurich. It became, alongside Lutheranism, a distinctive and influential strand of the Reformation. Yet it was exportable in a way that Lutheranism was not.

Through the influence of the refugees from persecution who lived for a while in Geneva, and the translation of his works from Latin and French, especially into English, Calvin's influence was internationalised. His theological outlook – 'Calvinism' – came to be a philosophy in more than one sense: a way of living, a view of the world, a distinctive ethos, a faith. According to Calvin's most recent biographer, Bernard Cottret, 'Calvinism' and 'Calvinist' first came to be used (in 1552) by the Lutheran Joachim Westphal in one of his controversial writings on the Supper, no doubt to denote John Calvin's distinctive view of the Lord's presence.[3]

Calvin deplored its use. But given his singular influence, that use became inevitable, quickly coming to have a wider connotation than his view of the Supper, a connotation acquired by the stream of Reformed confessions and catechisms that flowed not only from Geneva but also from other centres. Though Calvinism was widely influential, in a sense the meaning of 'Calvinism' became narrower, focussing on the distinctives of Calvin's soteriology, its edges sharpened by later controversies with Arminians and Socinians, as well as with the Roman Catholic Counter-Reformation. Many among

Episcopalians, Baptists and Independents, all people who disavowed Calvin's presbyterian church polity, were happy to be known as 'Calvinistic' or as 'doctrinal Calvinists'. Calvin was not only a consolidator of much of the work of Martin Luther and others. By emphasising the sufficiency and clarity of Scripture, the 'Word of God', in all matters of Christian belief and practice, he established the principle of *sola scriptura* as the basis of theologising. It was this method, as much as anything else, that his earnest followers carried forward sometimes with as much zeal but with fewer nuances than their teacher. Through appreciation of its biblical and systematic qualities, and (as Calvin himself would have said, and his followers did say) 'by the singular grace of God', the Reformed Faith became established. It was taken across the European mainland (the German states, the Low Countries, France, (until it was largely eliminated through persecution), Hungary, and to a lesser degree in Italy, Spain and Poland, places that were all subject to the later suppression of the Reformed faith. It was chiefly through its influence in the British Isles and Holland that, through its offspring, Puritanism, and what is today referred to as 'Reformed Orthodoxy', Calvinism spread to North America and to other non-European destinations.

My aim in this final chapter is to provide something of the intellectual flavour and abiding interest of this later 'Calvinism'. Glancing at three different strands in Calvinism – we could have looked at many others – will enable us to touch on some of the various ways in which Calvinism became established and then 'developed'. We shall sketch and assess one fairly straightforward 'development' of Calvin's theology, then look at one (of several) current scholarly debates about 'Calvin and the Calvinists', and finally note the way in which Calvin's thought has become significant in contemporary philosophy through 'Reformed' epistemology.

COVENANT THEOLOGY

Calvin had a very strong sense of the theological unity of Scripture, and especially of the unity of the two Testaments. What they have in common is greater than what divided them, for they plot the progress of one divine economy of grace begun shortly after the Fall and identifiable in successive eras through Abraham, Moses, David and the prophets. This succession culminated in the Incarnation, ministry, death and resurrection of Jesus Christ, the answer to the prayers of a faithful remnant of the Old Testament and the fulfilment of their prophecies.

> All whom, from the beginning of the world, God adopted as his peculiar people, were taken into covenant with him on the same conditions, and under the same bond of doctrine, as ourselves . . . it is of no small importance to establish this point.[4]

There were clear discontinuities between the Testaments as well, of course. In particular, at the Incarnation the Jewish theocracy came to an end, the Levitical law was superseded, and through the apostolic preaching the privileges of God's grace were extended beyond the Jewish people. Through Christ all peoples of the earth would be blessed. So for Calvin, the Manger, Calvary and Pentecost were not discontinuous, intrusive events; they completed the trajectory of the Old Testament. As we saw earlier, it is this sense of unity and continuity that enabled him to invoke aspects of the political arrangements of the Old Testament to inform (though not to be a blueprint for) his idea of Christian magistracy in Geneva.

So the covenant between God and man, the device through which God by his promise binds himself to Abraham at first and through him to a chosen people, to be their defender and Saviour, is one covenant differing only its various dispensations. 'The covenant made with all the fathers is so far from differing from ours in reality and substance, that it is altogether one and the same: still the administration differs'.[5] In both dispensations believers had the hope of immortality, the covenant was established not by their merits but by God's grace; and finally, Christ is revealed as the Mediator of this covenant.[6]

In the 1570s and 1580s the covenant motif was extended by certain Reformation theologians (e.g. Zacharias Ursinus (1534–83) and Caspar Olevianus (1538–87) of Heidelberg, and Robert Rollock (1555–99) of Edinburgh) to become a controlling theological idea, alongside a more scholastic development of the various topics of Reformed theology. For such 'covenant theologians' the covenant became the chief tool in interpreting Scripture, enabling people readily to identify the cause of the Reformation with that of Old Testament heroes and their enemies with the villains.

More interestingly, perhaps, the original arrangements made by the Lord with Adam also came to be regarded as covenantal. So with

Adam was made a covenant of *works*, which, upon the Fall, the covenant of *grace* superseded; and Christ the last Adam, prefigured in the Old Testament, and at work then in various ways, is the Mediator of this new covenant. Most interestingly of all, not only is the covenant motif extended to govern all the divine–human dispensations, prelapsarian and post-lapsarian, but also the covenant of grace is seen as the historical outworking of an eternal *pactum salutis* made between Father, Son and Spirit, the economic working of the Trinity. According to this scheme God the Father covenanted to elect an untold number of men and women and boys and girls to salvation, God the Son covenanted to redeem men and women by his death, and God the Spirit covenanted to apply the merits of Christ's work to the people of God. So election is assigned primarily to the Father, reconciliation to the Son and the application of that redemption to the Spirit. The three persons being the three persons of the one God, there is no tension or disharmony between these various roles, but each contributes to the glory of God in the salvation of the church.

This theology found later expression in the work of the Dutch theologians Johannes Cocceius (1603–69) and Herman Witsius (1636–1708), and in numerous other theologians such as the Englishman John Ball (1585–1640), and was given precise confessional expression in the Westminster Confession of Faith (1647). The idea of the covenant extended into politics, as in the Solemn League and Covenant (1643). So it became influential if not dominant wherever that Confession was influential and found many popular expositions, as in Thomas Boston's (1713–67), *Human Nature in its Fourfold State*.

This methodical arrangement of the biblical revelation under the overarching concept of the covenant has a number of pedagogic advantages. The resulting theology has one readily understandable theme and a number of variations. Covenanting is the activity of people: the three persons of the Trinity agreeing together in the covenant of redemption, the Lord establishes a covenant with Abraham, and so on. Such theology is conveyed not in abstract categories (such as election, predestination, redemption, grace) but in personal terms: promising, trusting, obeying, sending, giving and redeeming.

Is such covenant theology a legitimate development of Calvin's theology? Perhaps it is, if by that question is meant, would Calvin have become a covenant theologian had he lived longer? Yet while this question is not pure speculation, it is fairly speculative. What we know for certain is that while Calvin's theology is broadly covenantal in the way already described, there are important aspects of it that the more developed covenant theology is at odds with. So in order to have become a fully fledged covenant theologian, Calvin would have had to have changed his mind on some of these matters and made up his mind on others. We can mention them briefly.

First, Calvin has no conception of the covenant of works. It receives little or no treatment in the *Institutes*, and in his Genesis commentary he is silent on the matter. All he says is that if Adam had remained upright he would have gained the gift of perseverance and a 'primal and simple knowledge' of God would have ensued. There is no suggestion that the Lord made a covenant with Adam, or even that the Lord's relations with Adam are best understood in that way. Rather, had there be no Fall, the race would have enjoyed an orderly progression in the knowledge of God, a 'simple and primitive knowledge, to which the mere course of nature would have conducted us, had Adam stood upright'.[7]

Nor does he develop Paul's Adam–Christ parallel (Rom. 5.1 Cor. 15) in a covenantal direction. The idea, which had a tendency to creep into covenant theology, that in some sense Adam would have *merited* what would follow had he remained upright, would have been abhorrent to Calvin. One imagines, too, that he would have had to be persuaded that the idea of an eternal, inter-Trinitarian, covenant of redemption was a legitimate piece of 'accommodation'.

Second, what of Adam's relation to the race? When the covenant theologians pressed the parallel between Christ and Adam, it became natural for them to think of Christ and Adam exercising their respective covenantal roles in representative capacities. For, as the Adam–Christ parallel developed, it was odd to suppose that those who are redeemed by Christ are metaphysically one with him as the race is one in Adam in the Augustinian scheme. Such a direct parallel is not plausible even if one stresses the idea of personal union with Christ, as Calvin did.

In developed covenant theology, it became natural to think as follows: as Christ was the representative of his people, so was Adam the representative of the race. But perhaps though covenant theology and a representative relationship between Adam and the race have gone together, they do not *need* to go together. Perhaps one might tolerate an inexact parallel between Adam and Christ at this point.

What did Calvin himself think on this matter? The evidence is not altogether clear. Being an Augustinian as he was, we might expect

Calvin to have held Augustine's view, the view that Adam in his own person encapsulated the race, that the race was metaphysically one thing in Adam, so that when Adam fell the human race, being 'in him', fell too. In the *Institutes* he says that Adam is not a simply a single person, that the command of God not to eat of the tree tested his obedience,[8] that to treat Adam simply as an individual person is Pelagian,[9] and that in Adam the race lost righteousness and in Christ that righteousness is recovered and communicated.[10]

But he does not commit himself to a more precise view of the relationship of the race in Adam beyond saying that all are made guilty by the guilt of one who is the 'root of human nature'.[11] There are words in his Romans *Commentary* that seem to be deliberately ambiguous: 'For as Adam at his creation had received for us as well as for himself the gifts of God's favour, so by falling away from the Lord, he in himself corrupted, vitiated, depraved, and ruined our nature.'[12]

However, there is an interesting short section in his *Sermons on Galatians* in which he states, somewhat speculatively you may think, that God could have created us stronger and more perfect than he chose to, and that God could have ensured that only Adam fell.[13] This suggests a rather fuzzy understanding of Adam's role, but one that tends in a non-Augustinian direction, since if God could have ensured that only Adam fell then it cannot be that the race is really 'in Adam'. Calvin seems to allow that it is possible that Adam need not even have represented the race. On the other hand, perhaps not too much emphasis ought to be given to one paragraph in one sermon.

This brief discussion illustrates the general difficulty of making clear judgments, based upon an extrapolation of Calvin's ideas as they are found in his various writings, as to whether he would have endorsed this or that theological development that occurred within the Reformed community after his death. There is the ever-present danger of anachronism, and often, as in the case of Calvin and covenant theology, the evidence drawn from what Calvin wrote does not point uniformly in one direction.

THE KENDALL THESIS

Many scholars have argued that after Calvin Reformed theology quickly degenerated into scholasticism and rationalism. Sometimes the charge is that the degeneracy was a moral one, into legalism and moralism. But as Richard Muller and others have forcefully argued, many of these accusations are vague and ill-informed and also partisan. They routinely confuse method with doctrinal substance and outlook. They begin from a view of Calvin as a wholly biblical theologian, unaffected by philosophy and certainly by scholasticism. But as we have seen the evidence (as one would expect) points to Calvin being a child of his time, and that his thought was moulded by a variety of influences, including a somewhat eclectic use of ancient philosophy and of scholastic patterns of argumentation. The charge of degeneracy also fails to take into account the changed circumstances that quickly followed after Calvin's death.[14]

After Calvin there arise new theological challenges which had to be addressed, notably Socinianism, which can be regarded, in its attitude to the Bible, as deliberately naive and Biblicist, and in its attitude to Christian dogma, as sceptical and rationalistic. And alongside this was the onset of Arminianism, a re-birth of semi-Pelagianism within the Reformed constituency, which was (initially at least) expressed in scholastic terms. 'Scholasticism' was not the private preserve of Reformed orthodoxy.

Also, the Reform movement began as a protest movement against Roman corruption and infidelity to Scripture, holding out some hope, however fleeting, that the Church of Rome may be reformed from within. But prompted by the success of the Council of Trent and the rise of the Counter-Reformation, and weakened by the effects of physical persecution by the Church of Rome and her agents, the Reformation Protest transmuted into a rival church or set of churches.

In the generation that immediately followed Calvin, it became urgently necessary to educate a rising generation of Reformed ministers. Theology moved to the classroom and the lecture theatre, and a theological and philosophical curriculum was established. Attention had urgently to be given to theological method and the relation between theology and other disciplines, notably philosophy. The Counter-Reformation, which itself encompassed conflicts within the Jesuit order, between Jesuits and Dominicans, and with the Jansenists that mirrored the Calvinistic conflict with Arminianism, unintentionally (and rather ironically) bequeathed, through its Dominican and Jansenist parties, invaluable conceptual tools that enabled the Reformed to withstand Arminianism. For these reasons, after the death of Calvin Reformed theology quickly entered a new era of some complexity.

One instance of the tendency to see all this as a decline and fall is R. T. Kendall's *Calvin and English Calvinism to 1649*.[15] In fact Kendall makes a stronger claim, that Calvin's theology was actually reversed and *opposed* by what was ostensibly a Calvinistic movement, English Puritanism. It is worth sketching a part Kendall's thesis in a little detail and offering a brief assessment of it. He claims, as so many scholars of Calvin and Calvinism have done, that it was Calvin's immediate successor, Theodore Beza, who was responsible for initiating the reversal, and that the Puritans and Reformed scholastics took their cue from him.[16]

One place where this occurred, according to Kendall, is in the overturning of what he alleges to be Calvin's view, that assurance is an essential part of faith. Kendall claims that Calvin rejected the idea of definite atonement, the view that Christ's death, although sufficient for the redemption of everyone, was in fact intended only for some, for the elect. As a consequence a person is not plagued with the question of whether he or she is one of those for whom Christ died; self-examination and introspection ('Am I one of those for whom Christ died?') play no role in Calvin's view of faith, which is a simple reliance on the word of God.

But Kendall claims that in Puritan hands, due to the innovation of the doctrine of definite atonement, faith and assurance become separated, whereas in Calvin they were essentially connected. As a result Puritanism became an experimental, introspective religion in which the reality of one's faith had continually to be tested and assured. Legalism, doubt and fear ensued. It could no longer be taken for granted that true faith is assured faith. Here is some of what Kendall says: first about the extent of the atonement and then about faith and assurance.

> Fundamental to the doctrine of faith in John Calvin is his belief that Christ died indiscriminately for all men. Equally crucial, however, is his conviction that, until faith is given, 'all that he has suffered and done for the salvation of the human race remains useless and of no value for us'.[17]

Accordingly, faith comes only to the elect, a subset of those for whom Christ died.

What the elect are given, then, is a 'measure' of faith out of Christ's infinite bounty. This measure of faith is none the less fully assuring in its 'first and principal parts'. 'When first even the least drop of faith is instilled in our minds, we begin to contemplate God's face, peaceful and calm and gracious towards us. We see Him afar off, but so clearly as to know we are not at all deceived.' Calvin defines faith as 'a firm and certain knowledge of God's benevolence toward us, founded upon the truth of the *freely given promise in Christ*, both revealed to our minds and sealed upon our hearts through the Holy Spirit.'[18]

In assessing this there is first the question of Calvin's view of the atonement. Kendall writes as if Calvin himself is a participant in the complex debates that followed his death, with the rise of Amyraldianism and Arminianism, and controversies about the intended effect of the death of Christ. But in fact Calvin's views on these matters were undeveloped by comparison with what came after, simply because he was not faced with the later issues and forced to come to a view on them. So it is anachronistic to attempt to measure Calvin's various statements about the atonement against what came later. The most we can ask is whether Calvin's views are consistent with what came later.

As regards the nature of faith, if we test what Kendall says about faith and assurance by the text of the *Institutes*, what do we find? We have already seen that Calvin defines faith in terms of assurance. One might think that this settles the matter in Kendall's favour. But we noted in Chapter 6 that Calvin has much more to say, even in the very same passage. For example,

So deeply rooted in our hearts is unbelief, so prone are we to it, that while all confess with the lips that God is faithful, no man ever believes it without an arduous struggle.[19]

Calvin goes on to identify two dangers: the danger of despair, and because faith may be temporary there is the opposite danger of presumption.[20] He says this about temporary faith.

For though none are enlightened into faith, and truly feel the efficacy of the Gospel, with the exception of those who are foreordained to salvation, yet experience shows that the reprobate are sometimes affected in a way similar to the elect, that even in their own judgment there is no difference between them. Hence it is not strange, that by the Apostle a taste of heavenly gifts, and by Christ himself a temporary faith, is ascribed to them. Not that they truly perceive the power of spiritual grace and the sure light of faith; but the Lord, the better to convict them, and leave them without excuse, instils into their minds such a sense of his goodness as can be felt without the Spirit of adoption.[21]

And about presumption

It is one thing, in order to prevent believers from indulging vain confidence, to repress the temerity which, from the remains of the flesh, sometimes gains upon them, and it is another thing to strike terror into their consciences, and prevent them from feeling secure in the mercy of God.[22]

Because of these possibilities there is the need and duty for the believer to engage in self-examination. 'Meanwhile, believers are taught to examine themselves carefully and humbly, lest carnal security creep in and take the place of assurance of faith.'[23]

We see then that Calvin's account of faith contained various strands, and is more complex and nuanced than his definition, taken by itself, might lead us to think. Calvin is firm and clear in teaching that Christ (alone) is the mirror of God's election, and we thus discover the truth that we are elect not by reasoning a priori, by attempting to peer into the depths of God's secret plan, but by examining our relationship with Christ and especially whether or not we have the evidence of true faith in him. Each of these strands figured prominently in later Puritan pastoral theology. Such evidence suggest continuity rather than the degeneracy that Kendall claims.

In the space available it is not possible to go into the consequences for the unity and consistency of the account of Calvin's theology that Dr Kendall provides.[24] Nevertheless I hope to have shown that while in some instances, as in the case of covenant theology, one might hesitate to say that this is forthrightly Calvinian, in the case of faith and assurance, the possibility of presumption, or of despair, and consequently the need for self-examination and thus of 'experimental religion', it is reasonable on the evidence to conclude that, despite obvious differences elsewhere, here at least Calvin and Puritanism stand on more or less the same ground.

'REFORMED' EPISTEMOLOGY

For our last example of the influence of Calvin on later thought we turn from the theological debates of four centuries ago to those of contemporary epistemology, which may at first sight seem rather surprising. Yet as we noted in Chapter 1, Calvin's views on the *sensus divinitatis* have aroused considerable philosophical interest in recent years in connection with the articulation of 'Reformed' epistemology. Central to it is the contention that a person is within his epistemic rights to take the proposition 'God exists' and other fundamental claims about God as part of the foundations of his beliefs. No one has the obligation, in behaving rationally, to derive beliefs about God only from other beliefs which are self-evident to everyone. It is argued that such a requirement is not itself self-evidently true. It is not self-evidently true that belief in God is rational only if it is based upon what is self-evident.

More interestingly for us, it is also claimed that the seeds of this entitlement to hold that God exists (and other similar beliefs) without argument are to be found in what Calvin says about the universal *sensus divinitatis* in Book I of the *Institutes*. Alvin Plantinga, the leading 'Reformed' epistemologist, cites these words from *Institutes* I.5.1.

Lest anyone, then, be excluded from access to happiness, he not only sowed in men's minds that seed of religion of which we have spoken but revealed himself and daily discloses himself in the whole workmanship of the universe. As a consequence, men cannot open their eyes without being compelled to see him.

And then he draws the following conclusion

Calvin's claim is that one who accedes to this tendency and in these circumstances accepts the belief that God has created the world – perhaps upon beholding the starry heavens, or the splendid majesty of the mountains, or the intricate, articulate beauty of a tiny flower – is entirely within his epistemic rights in so doing. It is not that such a person is justified or rational in so believing by virtue of having an implicit argument – some version of the teleo-logical argument, say. No; he does not need any argument for justification or rationality. His belief need not be based on any other propositions at all; under these conditions he is perfectly rational in accepting belief in God in the utter absence of any argument, deductive or inductive. Indeed, a person in these condi-tions, says Calvin, *knows* that God exists.[25]

'Reformed' epistemology takes encouragement from the belief that in Calvin one finds very little attention given to the proofs of God's existence. There is little interest in developing a natural theology, and according to Calvin no requirement that a person ought to be able to prove that God exists, or to have that proof made by another on his behalf, in order for his belief in God's existence to be rational.

There is one possible explanation for Calvin's relative disinterest in natural theology that the 'Reformed' epistemologists by and large do not canvass. This is that Calvin may have believed (as Thomas Aquinas seems to have believed) that while natural theology is *possible*, and that those who have sufficient time, inclination and intelligence may pursue it, it is not *necessary* in order to satisfactorily ground religious belief. Calvin may have taken this outlook for granted just as, in the hurly-burly of the Reformation, he took many other things for granted.

Whether or not this is plausible, Calvin was undoubtedly inter-ested in the natural knowledge of God, in the nature and the limits of the *sensus divinitatis*. But there is little or no evidence that he is concerned about the *rationality* of belief in God of the kind that has preoccupied philosophers since the Enlightenment. Perhaps in his remarks about the *sensus divinitatis* he is not intending to provide us with the materials for constructing an alternative epistemology to strong foundationalism. Indeed, it is highly likely, for historical reasons, that he had no such intentions. His claim is not that strong foundationalism is wrong; to suppose so would be a gross anachronism. It is more radical than that: that since the noetic effects of sin are universal and, humanly speaking, are ineradicable, the recommended remedy is not the development of an alternative epis-temology but the knowledge of God the Redeemer freely given to us in Christ.

In criticism of Plantinga's appeal to Calvin's view of the *sensus divinitatis* Merold Westphal has noted,

Calvin would have put that last part rather differently, I suspect. In order to remind us that none of us come *naturally* to a proper knowledge of God, he would have said that while the tendency to believe is present, it is nevertheless suppressed, reversing Plantinga's order and emphasis. And in order to remind us that *none* of us comes naturally to a proper knowledge of God, he would have said that while the tendency to believe is universally present, it is *universally* and not just partially, suppressed. Both terms are ambiguous and might miss his meaning. Universal suppression might be construed as degree rather than extension, suggesting that creation is entirely obliterated rather than that none of us is exempt from the distorting effects of sin. Partial suppression might be construed as extension rather than degree, suggesting that some of us are exempt rather than that our natural tendency to believe in God has been distorted but not obliterated. I do not doubt that Calvin would rather risk overstating the damage by speaking of universal suppression than risk suggesting that some are exempt from the noetic effects of sin by speaking of a partial suppression.[26]

This seems to be fair comment, knowing as we do of the way in which Calvin thinks that sin has affected the *sensus*. Allied to this is a rather different difficulty, that in Calvin's treatment of the *sensus divinitatis* there is little or no interest in the rationality of religious belief. Rather, Calvin's interest in knowledge is in establishing that since all men and women have some knowledge of God, they are culpable when they do not form their lives in a way that is appropriate to such knowledge.

For how can the idea of God enter your mind without instantly giving rise to the thought, that since you are his workmanship, you are bound, by the very law of creation, to submit to his authority? – that your life is due to him? – that whatever you do ought to have reference to him?[27]

Since God himself, to prevent any man from pretending ignorance, has endued all men with some idea of his Godhead, the memory of which he constantly renews and occasionally enlarges, that all to a man, being aware that there is a God, and that he is their Maker, may be condemned by their own conscience when they neither worship him nor consecrate their lives to his service.[28]

In asserting the universality of the *sensus divinitatis*, Calvin is making the claim that as a matter of fact everyone has in them the seed of religion. And, following Paul in Romans 1, he is more concerned with using this fact about knowledge to establish the *responsibility* of all people in the sight of God for the use to which they put this knowledge than he is about saying anything about *rationality* or warrant. The point about foundationalism, whether weak or strong, is as Plantinga says about epistemic entitlement. But as we have seen Calvin says little or nothing about this, and he may imply little or nothing about it as well.

Those who look to Calvin as the *origo* of 'Reformed' epistemology (understood as a form of epistemological internalism) are in something of a dilemma at this point. If they appeal to him to provide a premise of a factual kind about the seed of religion working in all people, then they will certainly find evidence for this in Calvin, as we have seen. But it does not follow from Calvin's remarks about the presence of the seed of religion that a person is entitled to basically believe in God, to have that belief in one's noetic foundations. If on the other hand the 'Reformed' epistemologists appeal to a normative proposition as a premise, a proposition about what men and women ought to believe, which they would find warrant for in Calvin's remarks about the responsibility of all men and women before God, it is surely implausible to suppose that such a proposition is acceptable without reason or argument. Part of the problem with appealing to Calvin is that his remarks about the *sensus divinitatis* are first-order observations. He does not theorise about what he takes to be straightforward matters of fact.

More recently, 'Reformed' epistemologists have modified this view somewhat. 'Reformed' epistemology in its first phase saw Calvin's doctrine of the *sensus divinitatis* as warranting a case for permitting belief in God to be in the foundations of a person's noetic structure, and so properly basic for that person. More recently they have come to see the *sensus* as a mechanism which, when properly functioning, and in a propitious environment, produces true beliefs, foremost among which is the true belief that God exists. So Alvin Plantinga says that

The basic idea, I think, is that there is a kind of faculty or a cognitive mechanism, what Calvin calls a *sensus divinitatis* or sense of divinity, which in a wide variety of circumstances produces in us beliefs about God. These circumstances, we might say, trigger the disposition to form the beliefs in question; they form the occasion on which those beliefs arise. Under these circumstances, we develop or form theistic beliefs – or, rather, these beliefs are formed in us; in the typical case we don't consciously choose to have those beliefs. Instead, we find ourselves with them, just as we find ourselves with perceptual and memory beliefs.[29]

This more recent, externalist interpretation of Calvin's remarks on the *sensus divinitatis* seems nearer to what Calvin has in mind. Calvin's remarks seem to lend themselves to a more structural or mechanistic account of belief production, belief in God being triggered and renewed by the *sensus* as it is 'fed' by fresh data, 'fresh drops' as Calvin puts it, from the world around. On this proposal epistemology is not so much (to use Quine's word) 'naturalised', as 'supernaturalised', and normative questions about what we ought to believe, and the grounds we ought to have in order for those beliefs to be regarded as rational, give way to broadly factual questions about the nature of human cognitive mechanisms and hypotheses about the reasons for their malfunctioning. These questions include what constitutes proper functioning and also what counts as a 'normal' or 'natural' environment, questions which although factual are very difficult to settle to the satisfaction of all parties.

In his major work on religious epistemology, *Warranted Christian Belief*, Alvin Plantinga has gone even further. He has extended his externalist interpretation of Calvin's *sensus divinitatis* to Calvin's doctrine of the internal testimony of the Holy Spirit, (and to what Thomas Aquinas has to say about the 'instigation' or 'instinct' of the Holy Spirit),[30] seeing this as a forerunner or an exemplar of his own defence of the belief that the Scriptures are the Word of God.

What is required for *knowledge* is that a belief be produced by cognitive faculties or processes that are working properly, in an appropriate epistemic environment . . . according to a design plan that is aimed at truth, and is furthermore *successfully* aimed at truth. But according to this model (viz. the 'Extended

Aquinas/Calvin model') what one believes by faith (the beliefs that constitute faith) meets these four conditions.

First, when these beliefs are accepted by faith and result from the internal instigation of the Holy Spirit, they are produced by cognitive processes working properly; they are not produced by way of some cognitive malfunction. Faith, the whole process that produces them, is specifically designed by God himself to produce this very effect. . . . Second, according to the model, the maxi-environment in which we find ourselves, including the cognitive contamination produced by sin, is precisely the cognitive environment for which this process is designed. The typical minienvironment is also favorable. Third, the process is designed to produce *true* beliefs; and fourth, the beliefs it produces – belief in the great things of the gospel – are in fact true; faith is a reliable belief-producing process, so that the process in question is *successfully* aimed at the production of true beliefs.[31]

At this point Plantinga certainly echoes and endorses Calvin's position.

My Christian belief can have warrant, and warrant sufficient for knowledge, even if I don't know of and cannot make a good historical case for the reliability of the biblical writers or for what they teach. I don't *need* a good historical case for the truth of the central teachings of the gospel to be warranted in accepting them. . . . On the model, the warrant for Christian belief doesn't require that I or anyone else have this kind of historical information; the warrant floats free of such questions. It doesn't require to be validated or proved by some source of belief *other* than faith, such as historical investigation.[32]

Here Plantinga endorses Calvin's (and Aquinas's) estimate of the role of external proofs of the authority of Scripture as God's revelation that we discussed in earlier chapters. He cites Calvin in support of his belief that Scripture (through the work of the Holy Spirit) carries its own evidence with it, quoting from *Institutes* I.7.5 in support of this. He understands Calvin to be saying not that we have knowledge or certainty with respect to propositions such as *The Bible comes to us from the very mouth of God* or *The Book of Job is divinely inspired* but rather with respect to the actual teaching, the internal cognitive content of the Bible, we come to form the belief that it is the word of God. Nor does the idea of self-authentication mean that the believer sees that the Bible proves itself to be accurate or reliable. Nor, Plantinga thinks, is the certainty that the believer has with respect to such content, the certainty that comes from the propositions of the Bible being self-evidently true, which they aren't.

However, although the relevant propositions are not self-evidently true there are respects in which the truths of the gospel resemble self-evident truths, namely that they have their evidence immediately and not by inference from propositional evidence. Such evidence that the believer has of the divinity of the gospel he does not get from other propositions, and the direct evidence he has is of a degree and kind so as to confer warrant. This, according to Plantinga, is what Calvin means.[33] This account of Calvin's view of the internal testimony of the Holy Spirit is clear and perceptive.

There is this important difference between the case of the *sensus divinitatis* and that of the internal testimony of the Holy Spirit, however. The *sensus divinitatis*, whether understood as giving rise to the formation of the belief that God exists, a properly basic belief in the existence of God, or as a mechanism for the formation of true beliefs when it is operating properly and in a propitious environment, is according to Plantinga (and Calvin) a universal endowment of the human race. It is innate or concreated, though universally perverted by sin. By contrast, the belief that the Scriptures are the word of God, where this belief is formed by of the internal testimony of the Holy Spirit, is a *particular* endowment given only to some. It is the result of the sovereign intrusion of the Holy Spirit into the mind, when the mind is made aware of some central aspect of the Christian revelation, the articles of the faith. So it is an intrusion into the exercise of the cognitive capacities of some, not of all, men and women.

A FINAL WORD

The extent to which these various developments that we have been considering are deviations from or distortions of Calvin's position will no doubt be debated further. But highlighting identifiable differences between Calvin and later Calvinists should not blind us to the theology and spirituality that Calvin and the later Calvinists have in common. This is often obscured in current debate. After all,

John Calvin was the first Calvinist. So what, then, is Calvinism, understood in this sense?

Abraham Kuyper characterised Calvinism as the assertion of 'the sovereignty of the triune God over the whole cosmos',[34] producing the conviction that God is sovereign in every area of life. In his attempt to characterise Calvinism, the great twentieth century Princeton theologian, B. B. Warfield, changed the focus a little. He drew attention to some words of William James. In his *The Varieties of Religious Experience*. James wrote,

> The moralist must hold his breath and keep his muscles tense; and so long as this athletic attitude is possible all goes well – morality suffices. . . . There is a state of mind known to religious men, and to no others, in which the will to assert ourselves and hold our own has been displaced by a willingness to close our mouths and be as nothing in the floods and waterspouts of God. In this state of mind, what we most dreaded has become the habitation of our safety, and the hour of our moral death has turned into our spiritual birthday.[35]

Warfield commented,

> The psychological analyst has caught the exact distinction between moralism and religion. It is the distinction between trust in ourselves and trust in God. And when trust in ourselves is driven entirely out, and trust in God comes in, in its purity, we have Calvinism. Under the name of religion at its height, what Professor James has really described is therefore just Calvinism.[36]

NOTES

CHAPTER 1

1. Preface to *Commentary on the Psalms*, xl–xli. All quotations from Calvin's *Commentaries* are from the Calvin Translation Society edition. Further details are in the Bibliography.
2. There are a number of biographies of Calvin, beginning with the memoir by his colleague Theodore Beza (1565). Modern biographies include those by Jean Cadier (1960), T. H. L. Parker (1975), Alister McGrath (1990) and Bernard Cottret (1995). Further details will be found in the Bibliography.
3. *Calvin's Commentary on Seneca's De Clementia, with Introduction, Translation and Notes*, ed. F. L. Battles and A. M. Hugo (Leiden, E. J. Brill, 1969).
4. Preface, xlii.
5. *Inst.* III.4.1. trans. Henry Beveridge (Edinburgh, 1845, repr. London, James Clarke & Co. 1949). All quotations from the 1559 *Institutes* use this translation, of which there have been a number of printings. The latest is published by Hendrickson (Peabody, Mass., 2008).
6. 'Epistle to the Reader', *Institutes of the Christian Religion* (1559).
7. T. H. L. Parker, *Calvin's Doctrine of the Knowledge of God* (Grand Rapids, Mich., Eerdmans, 1959).
8. B. B. Warfield, 'Calvin's Doctrine of the Knowledge of God', *Calvin and Calvinism* (New York, Oxford University Press, 1931).
9. *Inst.* I.6.1.
10. *Inst.* I.1.1.
11. Jonathan Edwards, *The Freedom of the Will* (1758), ed. Paul Ramsey (New Haven, Yale University Press, 1957), 131.
12. Karl Barth and Emil Brunner, *Natural Theology,* trans. Peter Fraenkel (London, Geoffrey Bles, 1946).
13. Of course, one must not exaggerate. Although on this matter Barth sought to have Calvin as an ally, there are many other aspects of Calvin's theology to which he offered a sharp critique.
14. As T. H. L. Parker claims, *John Calvin* (Tring, Lion Publishing, 1987), 40.
15. *A Short History of Ethics* (London, Routledge, 1967, 123).
16. *Rational Theology and the Creativity of God* (Oxford, Blackwell, 1982, 172).
17. *Inst.* III.23.2.

18. *Inst.* I.13.3.
19. *Inst.* III.11.19.
20. *Inst.* III.15.2.
21. *Inst.* I. 15.6.
22. *Inst.* I.3.
23. For example, *Inst.* I.15.2, III.7.5, III.9.4.
24. *Inst.* II.2.18.
25. *Inst.* I.15.8.
26. See the discussion of self-contradiction in Paul Helm, *John Calvin's Ideas* (Oxford, Oxford University Press, 2004), 313–5, 354–60, 389–92.
27. For further discussion see Paul Helm, *Faith and Understanding* (Edinburgh, Edinburgh University Press, 1997).
28. We shall consider 'Reformed' epistemology further in Chapter 8.

CHAPTER 2

1. John Chrysostom (c.344/354–407). According to Stephen Benin, in Chrysostom's work 'the concept of accommodation and condescension acquire a role almost unequaled among the other fathers' (*The Footprints of God* (Albany, New York, SUNY Press, 1993) 56).
2. *Inst.* I.17.13.
3. *Inst.* I.1.1.
4. *The Confessions of Augustine,* trans. Henry Chadwick (Oxford, Oxford University Press, 1992) 180, 182.
5. Augustine, *Soliloquies,* in *Nicene and Post-Nicene Fathers Series I* v.7, ed. Philip Schaff (Grand Rapids, Mich., Eerdmans, 1980), 2.32.
6. *The Character of Theology* (Grand Rapids, Baker, 2005), 14.
7. *Inst.* I.1.1.
8. *Inst.* I.1.2.
9. *Inst.* II.1.1 See also II.2.10.
10. *Inst.* II.1.2.
11. *Inst.* II.1.3.
12. *Inst.* II.1.3.
13. *Inst.* I.3.1.
14. *Inst.* I.3.1.
15. *Inst.* I.2.1.
16. *Inst.* I.2.2.
17. *Inst.* I.4.1.
18. Marcus Tullius Cicero, *The Nature of the Gods,* trans. Horace C. P. McGregor (London, Penguin Books, 1972), 128.
19. *Inst.* II.2.22–3. Aristotle's accounts of the conditions of responsibility and of the relation between incontinence and intemperance are to be found in *Nicomachean Ethics,* Books III and VII respectively. See also Calvin's treatment of funeral practices as providing further evidence of the continuing effect of the *sensus* upon all societies. (*Inst.* III.25.5).
20. *Inst.* I.6.1.
21. *Inst.* I.5.1.
22. *Inst.* I.6.1.

23. *Inst.* I.6.1.
24. *Inst.* I.7.5.
25. *Inst.* I.7.
26. *Inst.* I.8.1.
27. *Summa Theologiae* Ia 1.6 (trans. Thomas Gilby).
28. Calvin is here endorsing a long tradition. For example, Duns Scotus offers some of the very same arguments which Calvin uses (e.g. the internal concordance or consistency of Scripture and the fact that Scripture contains divinely attested miracles). Like Calvin, he thinks that such arguments are rationally compelling, but that they fall short of a proof. (On this, see Richard Cross, *Duns Scotus* (New York, Oxford University Press, 1999) 12).
29. *Inst.* I.8.13.
30. *Inst.* I.7.4.
31. *Inst.* I.7.5.
32. *Inst.* III.2.14. This passage is taken from Calvin's treatment of faith.
33. *Inst.* III.2.15.
34. *Inst.* III.2.
35. *Inst.* I.7.5.

CHAPTER 3

1. For Aquinas, see, for example, *Summa Theologiae* Ia, 11–12.
2. *Inst.* I.13.2.
3. *Inst.* I.13.20.
4. *Inst.* III.21.5.
5. *Comm.* Ps.77.14.
6. *Inst.* I.10.2.
7. See *Comm.* Psalm 77.9 and Daniel. 9.9, for example.
8. *Comm.* Zephaniah 1.12.
9. *Inst.* I.13.1. Writing of the Second Commandment he says it 'restrains our license from daring to subject God, who is incomprehensible, to our sense perceptions, or to represent him by any form.' (*Inst.* II.8.17).
10. *Inst.* I.13.21 The passage from Hilary of Poitiers (c.315–368) reads, 'Leave to God the privilege of knowing himself; for it is he only who is able to bear witness to himself who knows himself by himself alone. And we shall be leaving him what belongs to him if we understand him as he declares himself, and ask nothing at all concerning him except through his word.' (*On the Trinity*, I. xviii, Quoted in F. Wendel, *Calvin: The Origins and Development of His Religious Thought* (London, Fontana Library, 1965), 152)
11. *Inst.* I.13.18.
12. Saint Hilary of Poitiers, *The Trinity*, trans. Stephen McKenna, C.SS.R. (Washington D.C., Catholic University Press, 1954), II.2.
13. *Inst.* I.13.5.
14. *On the Trinity*, VII.IV.7, trans. A. W. Haddan (Edinburgh, T&T Clark, 1873).

15. *Inst.* I.13.5.
16. *Inst.* I.13.18.
17. *Inst.* I.13.5.
18. Calvin refers to Servetus and alludes to Gentile in *Inst.* I.13.22–23 and to Blandrata in *Inst.* I.13.2.
19. *Inst.* I.13.23.
20. *Inst.* I.13.24.
21. Quoted by B. B. Warfield, 'Calvin's Doctrine of the Trinity' in *Calvin and Calvinism* (208–9) from Calvin's *Adversus Petri Caroli* (1545).
22. Warfield, 'Calvin's Doctrine of the Trinity', 206.
23. Quoted by Warfield, 'Calvin's Doctrine of the Trinity' in *Calvin and Calvinism*, 210.
24. For example, *Inst.* I.13.4; I.13.7; I.13.23; I.13.24.
25. *Inst.* I.13.17.
26. *Inst.* I.13.20.
27. *Institution of the Christian Religion* (1536) trans. F. L. Battles (Atlanta, John Knox Press, 1975), chapter 2. S. 7, 8, 9.
28. *Inst.* I.13.19.
29. *Comm.* John 15.26.
30. *Inst.* I.13.14–5.
31. *Inst.* I.13.8.
32. *Inst.* I.13.2.
33. Karl Barth, *Church Dogmatics* II.2 (Edinburgh, T&T Clark, 1956), 64.
34. *Inst.* II.17.1.
35. Calvin, *Comm.* on Hebrews 1.3.
36. *Concerning the Eternal Predestination of God* (1552) trans. with an Introduction by J. K. S. Reid (London, James Clarke, 1961), 150. Cf.,127. See also *Comm.* John 13.18.
37. *Inst.* II.12.1.
38. *Inst.* II.12.7.
39. *Inst.* II.12.2.
40. Karl Rahner, *On the Trinity*, trans. J. Donceel (New York, Herder and Herder, 1970) 22, 34.
41. Barth, *Church Dogmatics*, II.2, 249.
42. T. F. Torrance, 'Calvin's Doctrine of the Trinity' (*Calvin Theological Journal*, 1990), 179.
43. Torrance, 'Calvin's Doctrine of the Trinity', 177, 178.
44. Torrance, 'Calvin's Doctrine of the Trinity', 179.
45. *John Calvin: Student of the Church Fathers* (Edinburgh, T&T Clark 1999), chapter 3.
46. Warfield, 'Calvin's Doctrine of the Trinity', 229–30.

CHAPTER 4

1. *Inst.* II.16.1.
2. *Inst.* II.15.1.
3. *Inst.* III.11.1.

4. John H. Leith ed. *Creeds of the Churches* (New York, Anchor, 1963), 36.
5. *Inst.* II.13.2.
6. *Comm.* John 1.14.
7. These expressions are taken from *Inst.* II.12 and 13.
8. See, for example *Inst.* II.14.1.
9. *Inst.* IV.17.30.
10. *Inst.* IV.17.30.
11. These rules are discussed further in *John Calvin's Ideas,* chapter 3.
12. *Inst.* II.14.3.
13. *Inst.* II.14.3.
14. *Inst.* II.2.4.
15. *Inst.* II.12.1.
16. *Inst.* II.12.7.
17. *Inst.* II.17.1.
18. *Inst.* II.12.3.
19. *Inst.* II 12.4.
20. *Inst.* II.12.1. See also *Comm.* Col. 1.20.
21. *Inst.* II.16.3.
22. Sermon on Gal. 1.3–5, *John Calvin's Sermons on Galatians* (trans. Kathy Childress, Edinburgh, Banner of Truth, 1997), 24.
23. *Sermons on Isaiah's Prophecy of the Death and Passion of Christ* (trans. and ed. T. H. L. Parker, London, James Clarke and Co. 1956), Isaiah, 53.4–6. See also *Comm.* John 15.13.
24. *Summa Theologiae*, 3a 1.2 trans. R. J. Hennessey. The quotation from Augustine is from *On the Trinity* 13.10.
25. *Inst.* II.12.1.
26. *Inst.* II.17.1.
27. Wendel, *Calvin: The Origins and Development*, 129.
28. *Inst.* II.12.3.
29. *Inst.* II.17.4.
30. For more on the penal substitutionary character of the atonement according to Calvin see Henri Blocher, 'The Atonement in John Calvin's Theology' in *The Glory of the Atonement,* ed. C. E. Hill and F. A. James III (Downers Grove, Ill., InterVarsity Press, 2004).
31. For example *Inst.* II.17.3–5.
32. *Inst.* III.16.1.
33. *Inst.* III.1.2.
34. *Inst.* III.11.15.
35. *Inst.* III.11.15.
36. *Inst.* III.16.1.
37. *Inst.* III.11.7.
38. *Inst.* III.11.2.
39. I recognise that this way of making the distinction between Christ's three offices is somewhat artificial, since for Calvin the priestly office of Christ continues in the present through his heavenly session and intercession for the Church. 'It belongs to a priest to *intercede* for the people, that they may obtain favour with God. This is what Christ is ever doing, for

it was for this purpose that he rose again from the dead. Then of right, for his continual intercession, he claims for himself the office of the priesthood.' (*Comm.* Hebrews 7.25).

CHAPTER 5

1. *Selected Works of John Calvin, Tracts and Letters*, ed. Henry Beveridge and Jules Bonnet (Grand Rapids, Mich., Baker, 1983), II.132.
2. *Comm.* I Cor. 1.30.
3. *Inst.* III.1.4.
4. *Inst.* III.15.2.
5. For more on this, see *John Calvin's Ideas*, Chapter 10.
6. For this idea, see *Comm.* Col. 1.20.
7. *Summa Theologiae*, Ia, 2ae, 114.1 trans. Cornelius Ernst.
8. *Inst.* III.17.8.
9. *Inst.* III.2.7.
10. *Inst.* III.2.4.
11. *Inst.* III.2.4.
12. *Inst.* III.2.19.
13. *Inst.* III.11.1.
14. For further discussion of the different senses of 'free will' according to Calvin, see *John Calvin's Ideas*, Chapter 6.
15. *The Bondage and Liberation of the Will* (1543) ed. Anthony N. S. Lane, trans. G. I. Davies (Grand Rapids, Mich., Baker, 1996).
16. *Inst.* III.21.7.
17. *Inst.* III.11.16.
18. *Inst.* III.21.5.
19. Thomas Aquinas, *Summa Theologiae*, 1a.23.
20. *Inst.* III.23.8.
21. *Inst.* III.24.12.
22. *Inst.* III.23.2.
23. *Inst.* III.21.7.
24. *Comm.* Rom. 11.2.
25. *Inst.* III.23.2.
26. *Inst.* III.23.4.
27. *Inst.* III.23.3.
28. *Inst.* I.16.2.
29. *Summa Theologiae*, Ia 22.2 trans. Thomas Gilby.
30. *Inst.* I.17.6.
31. *Inst.* II.4.2.
32. *Inst.* III.24.5.
33. Barth, *Church Dogmatics*, II. 2. 63.

CHAPTER 6

1. *Inst.* III.6.2.
2. *Inst.* III.6.5.
3. *Inst.* III.7.1.

4. *Inst.* III.6.3.
5. *Inst.* III.7.1.
6. *Inst.* III.6.5.
7. *Inst.* III.7.3.
8. *Inst.* II.8.5.
9. *Inst.* II.8.11.
10. *Inst.* II.8.1.
11. For a clear discussion of the Divine Command Theory as an epistemic thesis see Michael J. Harris, *Divine Command Ethics* (London, Routledge Curzon, 2003).
12. *Inst.* II.3.3.
13. *John Calvin's Sermons on the Ten Commandments*, trans. B. W. Farley (Grand Rapids, Mich, Baker, 1980) 189.
14. *John Calvin's Sermons on the Ten Commandments*, 247.
15. *Comm.* Genesis 2.3.
16. *Inst.* III.10.1.
17. *Inst.* IV.10.5.
18. *Inst.* IV.10.6.
19. *Inst.* IV.10.6.
20. *Inst.* III.10.2. See also III.10.3.
21. *Institution of the Christian Religion,* (1536). The translation is from T. H. L. Parker, *John Calvin*, 58–9.
22. *Inst.* III.10.4.
23. *Inst.* III.10.5
24. *Inst.* III.10.4.
25. *Inst.* III.10.1.
26. *John Calvin's Selected Works, Tracts and Letters*, III.
27. See John Witte Jr and Robert M. Kingdon (eds), *Sex, Marriage and Family in John Calvin's Geneva. Vol. I Courtship, Engagement and Marriage* (Grand Rapids, Mich., Eerdmans, 2005).
28. *Inst.* III.10.6.
29. John Calvin, *Sermons on the Beatitudes*, trans. Robert White (Edinburgh, Banner of Truth Trust, 2006), 43. The sermons were delivered in 1560.
30. For a detailed account of the creation of the *Bourse* and its growth in Calvin's time, see Jeannine E. Olson, *Calvin and Social Welfare* (Selinsgrove, Susquehanna University Press, 1989).
31. *Inst.* I.17.4.
32. *Defence of the Secret Providence of God* (1558) trans. Henry Cole in *Calvin's Calvinism* (London, Sovereign Grace Union, 1927), 236.
33. *Inst.* I.16 9.
34. *Inst.* I.17.1.
35. *Inst.* I.17.2–11.
36. *Inst.* III.9.1.
37. *Inst.* III.9.2.
38. *Inst.* III.9.2.
39. *Inst.* III.9.3.
40. *Inst.* III.9.4.

41. There is good evidence that Calvin suffered from a catalogue of illnesses, including abdominal pain, constipation and haemorrhoids, catarrh and coughing, kidney stones and gout. See the fascinating account in John Wilkinson, *The Medical History of the Reformers: Luther, Calvin and John Knox* (Edinburgh, Handsel Press, 2001). Note also Calvin's letter to the physicians of Montpellier, 8 February 1564, *Selected Works of John Calvin,* IV, 358.
42. *Inst.* III.9.5.

CHAPTER 7

1. *Inst.* IV.1.1. See also IV.1.4.
2. *Inst.* IV.1.1.
3. *Inst.* IV.1.27.
4. *Inst.* IV.1.7.
5. *Inst.* IV.2.1.
6. *Inst.* IV.2.11.
7. *Inst.* IV.2.11.
8. *Inst.* IV.2.12.
9. *Inst.* IV.14 1.
10. *Inst.* IV.14.4.
11. *Inst.* IV.17.14f.
12. *Inst.* IV.17.18.
13. *Inst.* IV.17.18.
14. *Inst.* IV.17.16.
15. *Inst.* IV.17.30.
16. *Inst.* IV.17.30.
17. *Inst.* IV.17.30.
18. *Comm.* on Ephesians 4.10.
19. *Inst.* IV.17.1.
20. *Inst.* IV.17.2.
21. *Inst.* IV.17.10.
22. *Inst.* IV.17.7.
23. *Inst.* IV.15.5.
24. *Inst.* IV.15.6.
25. *Inst.* IV.15.10.
26. *Inst.* IV.16.1.
27. *Canons and Decrees of the Council of Trent, with the Antidote* (1547) (*Selected Works, Tracts and Letters*), III.109–110.
28. *Inst.* IV.12.2.
29. *Inst.* III.4.14.
30. *Inst.* IV.12.10.
31. *Inst.* II.11.14.
32. *Inst.* IV.20.9.
33. *Inst.* IV.20.13.
34. *Inst.* IV.20.11.
35. *Inst.* IV.11.4.
36. *Inst.* IV.20.9.

37. *Inst.* IV.20.14.
38. *Inst.* IV.20.8.
39. *Inst.* IV.20.14.
40. *Inst.* IV.20.15.
41. *Inst.* IV.20.16.
42. *Commentary on a Harmony of the Gospels*, II.173, on Luke 14.23.
43. There is a fuller account of this correspondence in Bernard Cottret, *Calvin, A Biography*, 213–227.
44. *Selected Works, Tracts and Letters*, V. 33.
45. Pierre Bayle, *A Philosophical Commentary on These Words of the Gospel, Luke 14:23, 'Compel Them to Come in, That My House May Be Full'* (1686–8, trans. 1708. Edited with an Introduction, by John Kilcullen and Chandran Kukathas (Indianapolis, Liberty Fund, 2005)), 198.
46. *Inst.* IV.20.31.
47. *Inst.* IV.20.24.
48. *Inst.* IV.20.31.
49. *Inst.* III.19.15.
50. *Inst.* II.2.13. See also IV.20.2 and III.19.15.
51. 'Secular Authority: To What Extent It Should Be Obeyed' (1523), taken from John Dillenberger, *Martin Luther, Selections from His Writings and with an Introduction* (Garden City, New York, Anchor Books, 1961), 371.
52. *Commentary*, Genesis 4.20.
53. *Inst.* III.9.4.
54. *Inst.* III.9.5. See also III.25.2.

CHAPTER 8

1. Parker, *John Calvin*, 183.
2. The words of Theodore Beza, cited in Cottret, *Calvin, A Biography*, 262.
3. Cottret, *Calvin, a Biography*, 239.
4. *Inst.* II.10.1.
5. *Inst.* II.10.2.
6. *Inst.* II.10.2.
7. *Inst.* I 2.1.
8. *Inst.* II.1.4.
9. *Inst.* II.1.5.
10. *Inst.* II.1.6.
11. *Inst.* II.1.6.
12. *Commentary* on Romans 5.12.
13. *Sermons on Galatians*, 329–30.
14. Richard A Muller, *After Calvin* (New York, Oxford University Press, 2003).
15. Oxford, Clarendon Press, 1979.
16. Among recent, more balanced accounts of Beza are Jeffrey Mallinson, *Faith, Reason, and Revelation in Theodore Beza* (Oxford, Oxford University Press, 2003) and Shawn D. Wright, *Our Sovereign Refuge: The Pastoral Theology of Theodore Beza* (Carlisle, Paternoster Press, 2004).
17. Kendall, 13.

18. Kendall, 18. The first quotation is from *Inst.* III.2.19, the second from *Inst.* III.2.7 (italics added by Dr. Kendall).
19. *Inst.* III.2.15.
20. See Calvin's anatomising of the struggles and conflicts of faith *Inst.* III.2 17–21.
21. *Inst.* III.2.11.
22. *Inst.* III.2.22.
23. *Inst.* III.2.11.
24. For a fuller critical treatment, see Paul Helm, *Calvin and the Calvinists* (Edinburgh, Banner of Truth, 1988). Other treatments of Calvin which are sympathetic to the Kendall approach include Kevin Dixon Kennedy, *Union with Christ and the Extent of the Atonement* (New York, Peter Lang, 2002).
25. Alvin Plantinga, 'Reason and Belief in God' in *Faith and Rationality,* ed. Alvin Plantinga and Nicholas Wolterstorff (Notre Dame, University of Notre Dame Press, 1983), 67.
26. 'On Taking St. Paul Seriously: Sin as an Epistemological Category', in *Christian Philosophy*, ed. T. Flint. (Notre Dame, University of Notre Dame Press, 1990), 213.
27. *Inst.* I.2.2.
28. *Inst.* I.3.1.
29. *Warranted Christian Belief* (New York, Oxford University Press, 2000), 172–3. Plantinga also cites *Inst.* I.3.1. (171).
30. Aquinas, *Summa Theologiae*, 2a 2ae. 2.9 'One who believes does have a sufficient motive for believing, namely the authority of God's teaching, confirmed by miracles and – what is greater – the inner inspiration of God inviting him to believe. Thus he does not *give credit lightly'*. This passage is quoted by Plantinga, *Warranted Christian Belief*, 249 fn. 18.
31. Plantinga, *Warranted Christian Belief*, 256–7. Note that Plantinga's account presupposes the thoroughly Calvinian idea that faith is a form of knowledge.
32. Plantinga, *Warranted Christian Belief*, 259.
33. Plantinga, *Warranted Christian Belief*, 262.
34. Quoted by Peter S. Heslam, *Creating a Christian Worldview: Abraham Kuyper's Lectures on Calvinism* (Grand Rapids, Eerdmans, 1998), 114.
35. William James, *The Varieties of Religious Experience* (Edinburgh: Fount, 1977), 63–4.
36. 'What is Calvinism?' in *Selected Shorter Writings of Benjamin B. Warfield* Vol. I, ed. John E. Meeter (Nutley, New Jersey, Presbyterian and Reformed Publishing Company, 1970), 391.

BIBLIOGRAPHY

This Bibliography lists only items that have been used or are referred to in the present work. A more extensive bibliography may be found in *The Cambridge Companion to John Calvin*, ed. Donald K. McKim (Cambridge, Cambridge University Press, 2004). The *Calvin Theological Journal* regularly carries articles about Calvin, occasional new translations of Calvin material and an annual bibliographical survey covering all aspects of Calvin and Calvinism.

PRIMARY SOURCES

The Bondage and Liberation of the Will (1543), ed. A. N. S. Lane, trans. G. I. Davies (Grand Rapids, Mich., Baker, 1966)

Calvin's Calvinism, trans. Henry Cole (London, Sovereign Grace Union, 1927)

Calvin's Commentaries (Calvin Translation Society, Edinburgh 1843–55. Reprinted, Grand Rapids, Mich., Baker, 1979)

Calvin's Commentary on Seneca's De Clementia, With Introduction, Translation and Notes, ed. F. L. Battles and A. M. Hugo (Leiden, E.J. Brill, 1969)

Calvin's Selected Works, Tracts and Letters, ed. Henry Beveridge and Jules Bonnet (Grand Rapids, Mich., Baker, 1983)

Concerning the Eternal Predestination of God (1552), trans. J. K. S. Reid (London, James Clarke and Co., 1961)

Defence of the Secret Providence of God (1558), trans. Henry Cole in *Calvin's Calvinism* (London, Sovereign Grace Union, 1927)

Institutes of the Christian Religion (1559), trans. Henry Beveridge (Edinburgh, 1845, reprinted London, James Clarke & Co., 1949)

John Calvin, Treatises Against the Anabaptists and Against the Libertines, trans. and ed. B. W. Farley (Grand Rapids, Mich., Baker, 1982)

John Calvin's Sermons on Galatians, trans. Kathy Childress (Edinburgh, Banner of Truth, 1997)

John Calvin's Sermons on the Ten Commandments, trans. B. W. Farley (Grand Rapids, Mich., Baker, 1980)

Sermons on the Beatitudes, trans. Robert White (Edinburgh, Banner of Truth, 2006)

Sermons on Isaiah's Prophecy of the Death and Passion of Christ, trans. and ed. T. H. L. Parker (London, James Clarke and Co., 1956)

Sex, Marriage and Family in John Calvin's Geneva. Vol. I Courtship, Engagement and Marriage, ed. John Witte Jr and Robert M. Kingdon (Grand Rapids, Mich., Eerdmans, 2005)

SECONDARY SOURCES

Anselm of Canterbury, 'On the Incarnation of the Word' in *Anselm of Canterbury: The Major Works,* edited with an Introduction by Brian Davies and G. R. Evans (Oxford, Oxford University Press, 1998)

Aquinas, Thomas, *Summa Theologiae,* Latin text and English translation, various translators (Blackfriars, in conjunction with London: Eyre and Spttiswoode; New York, McGraw-Hill Book Company, 1963–80)

Aristotle, *Nichomachean Ethics,* trans. David Ross, revised by J. L. Ackrill and J. O. Urmson (Oxford, Oxford University Press, 1980)

Augustine, *On the Trinity,* trans. A. W. Hadden (Edinburgh, T&T Clark, 1873)

Augustine, *Soliloquies,* in *Nicene and Post-Nicene Fathers Series I,* Vol. 7, edited by Philip Schaff (Grand Rapids, Mich., Eerdmans, 1980)

Augustine, *Confessions,* trans. Henry Chadwick (Oxford, Oxford University Press, 1992)

Barth, Karl, *Church Dogmatics* II.2 (Edinburgh, T&T Clark, 1956)

Barth, Karl and Brunner, Emil, *Natural Theology,* trans. Peter Fraenkel (London, Geoffrey Bles, 1946)

Bayle, Pierre, *A Philosophical Commentary on These Words of the Gospel, Luke 14:23, 'Compel Them to Come in, that My House May be Full'* (1686), Edited with an Introduction by John Kilcullan and Chanda Kukathas (Indianapolis, Liberty Fund, 2005)

Bavinck, H. 'Calvin on Common Grace', *Princeton Theological Review,* 1909, 437–465.

Bavinck, H. 'Common Grace', trans. R. Van Leeuwen, *Calvin Theological Journal,* 1989, 35–65.

Benin, Stephen, *The Footprints of God* (Albany, New York, SUNY Press, 1993)

Beza, Theodore, 'The Life of John Calvin', in *Selected Works of John Calvin, Tracts and Letters,* edited by Henry Beveridge and Jules Bonnet (Grand Rapids Mich., Baker, 1983)

Blocher, Henri, 'Atonement in John Calvin's Theology' in *The Glory of the Atonement,* edited by C. E. Hill and F. A. James III (Downers Grove, Ill. InterVarsity Press, 2004)

Cadier, Jean, *The Man God Mastered,* trans. O. R. Johnston (London, IVP, 1960)

Cicero, *The Nature of the Gods,* trans. Horace C. P. McGregor (London, Penguin Books, 1972)

Cottret, Bernard, *Calvin, A Biography,* trans. M. Wallace McDonald (Edinburgh, T&T Clark, 2000)

Cross, Richard, *Duns Scotus* (New York, Oxford University Press, 1999)

Edwards, Jonathan, *The Freedom of the Will* (1758), edited by Paul Ramsey (New Haven, Yale University Press, 1957)

Franke, John R., *The Character of Theology* (Grand Rapids, Mich., Baker, 2005)

Gregory Nazianzus, 'Of Holy Baptism', in J. P. Migne, *Patrologie cursus completus, series Graeca*, Vol. 36.

Haas, Guenther, *The Concept of Equity in Calvin's Ethics* (Carlisle, Paternoster Press, 1997)

Harris, Michael J., *Divine Command Ethics* (London, RoutledgeCurzon, 2003)

Helm, Paul, *Calvin and the Calvinists* (Edinburgh, Banner of Truth, 1982)

Helm, Paul, *Faith and Understanding* (Edinburgh, Edinburgh University Press, 1997)

Helm, Paul, *John Calvin's Ideas* (Oxford, Oxford University Press, 2004)

Heslam, Peter S., *Creating a Christian Worldview: Abraham Kuyper's Lectures on Calvinism* (Grand Rapids, Mich., Eerdmans, 1998)

Hilary of Poitiers, *The Trinity*, trans. Stephen McKenna (Washington D.C., Catholic University Press, 1954)

James, William, *The Varieties of Religious Experience* (1902) (Glasgow, Collins Fount, 1960)

Kendall, R. T., *Calvin and English Calvinism to 1649* (Oxford, Clarendon Press, 1979)

Kennedy, J. D., *Union with Christ and the Extent of the Atonement* (New York, Peter Lang, 2002)

Kuiper, H., *Calvin on Common Grace* (Grand Rapids, Mich., Smitter Book Company, 1928)

Lane, Anthony N. S., *John Calvin: Student of the Church Fathers* (Edinburgh, T&T Clark, 1999)

Leith, John, *Creeds of the Churches* (Garden City, New York, Anchor Books, 1963)

Luther, Martin, *Selections from His Writings and with an Introduction by John Dillenberger* (Garden City, Anchor, 1961)

Macintyre, Alasdair C., *A Short History of Ethics* (London, Routledge, 1967)

Mallinson, Jeffrey, *Faith, Reason and Revelation in Theodore Beza* (Oxford, Oxford University Press, 2003)

McGrath, Alister, *A Life of John Calvin* (Oxford, Blackwell, 1990)

Muller, Richard A., *The Unaccommodated Calvin* (New York, Oxford University Press, 2000)

Muller, Richard A., *After Calvin* (New York, Oxford University Press, 2003)

Olson, Jeannine E., *Calvin and Social Welfare* (Selmsgrove, Susquehanna University Press, 1989)

Parker, T. H. L., *Calvin's Doctrine of the Knowledge of God* (Grand Rapids, Mich., Eerdmans, 1959)

Parker, T. H. L., *John Calvin* (Tring, Herts, Lion, 1987)

Peterson, Robert A., *Calvin and the Atonement* (2nd edn, Fearn, Ross-shire, Mentor, 1999)

Plantinga, Alvin, 'Reason and Belief in God', in *Faith and Rationality,* edited by Alvin Plantinga and Nicholas Wolterstorff (Notre Dame, University of Notre Dame University, 1983)

Plantinga, Alvin, *Warranted Christian Belief* (New York, Oxford University Press, 2000)

Rahner, Karl, *On the Trinity,* trans. J. C. Donceel (New York, Herder and Herder, 1970)

Torrance, T. F., 'Calvin's Doctrine of the Trinity', *Calvin Theological Journal* 25, (1990)

Van Buren, Paul, *Christ in Our Place* (Edinburgh, Oliver & Boyd, 1957)

Ward, Keith, *Rational Theology and the Creativity of God* (Oxford, Blackwell, 1982)

Warfield, B. B., 'John Calvin, the Man and His Work', in *Calvin and Calvinism* (New York, Oxford University Press, 1931)

Warfield, B. B., 'Calvin's Doctrine of the Knowledge of God', in *Calvin and Calvinism* (New York, Oxford University Press, 1931)

Warfield, B. B., 'Calvin's Doctrine of the Trinity', in *Calvin and Calvinism* (New York, Oxford University Press, 1931)

Warfield, B. B. 'What is Calvinism?', in *Selected Shorter Writings of Benjamin B. Warfield* Vol. I, edited by John E. Meeter (Nutley, NJ, Presbyterian and Reformed Publishing Company, 1970)

Wendel, François, *Calvin: The Origins and Development of his Religious Thought* (London, Collins, Fontana Library, 1965)

Westphal, Merold, 'On Taking St. Paul Seriously: Sin as an Epistemological Category', in *Christian Philosophy,* edited by T. Flint (Notre Dame, University of Notre Dame Press, 1990)

Wilkinson, John, *The Medical History of the Reformers: Luther, Calvin and John Knox* (Edinburgh, Handsel Press, 2001)

Willis, E. David, *Calvin's Catholic Christology* (Leiden, E.J. Brill, 1966)

Wright, Shawn D., *Our Sovereign Refuge: The Pastoral Theology of Theodore Beza* (Carlisle, Paternoster Press, 2004)

INDEX